T0311589

Cambridge Elements ☰

Elements in Language Teaching
edited by
Heath Rose
Linacre College, University of Oxford
Jim McKinley
University College London

ENGLISH-MEDIUM INSTRUCTION IN HIGHER EDUCATION

David Lasagabaster
University of the Basque Country UPV/EHU

CAMBRIDGE
UNIVERSITY PRESS

Shaftesbury Road, Cambridge CB2 8EA, United Kingdom

One Liberty Plaza, 20th Floor, New York, NY 10006, USA

477 Williamstown Road, Port Melbourne, VIC 3207, Australia

314–321, 3rd Floor, Plot 3, Splendor Forum, Jasola District Centre,
New Delhi – 110025, India

103 Penang Road, #05–06/07, Visioncrest Commercial, Singapore 238467

Cambridge University Press is part of Cambridge University Press & Assessment,
a department of the University of Cambridge.

We share the University's mission to contribute to society through the pursuit of
education, learning and research at the highest international levels of excellence.

www.cambridge.org
Information on this title: www.cambridge.org/9781108829052

DOI: 10.1017/9781108903493

© David Lasagabaster 2022

This publication is in copyright. Subject to statutory exception and to the provisions
of relevant collective licensing agreements, no reproduction of any part may take
place without the written permission of Cambridge University Press & Assessment.

First published 2022

A catalogue record for this publication is available from the British Library.

ISBN 978-1-108-82905-2 Paperback
ISSN 2632-4415 (online)
ISSN 2632-4407 (print)

Cambridge University Press & Assessment has no responsibility for the persistence
or accuracy of URLs for external or third-party internet websites referred to in this
publication and does not guarantee that any content on such websites is, or will
remain, accurate or appropriate.

English-Medium Instruction in Higher Education

Elements in Language Teaching

DOI: 10.1017/9781108903493
First published online: August 2022

David Lasagabaster
University of the Basque Country UPV/EHU

Author for correspondence: David Lasagabaster, david.lasagabaster@ehu.eus

Abstract: This Element focuses on English-Medium instruction (EMI), an educational approach that is spreading widely and rapidly in higher education institutions throughout the world because it is regarded as a linchpin of the internationalization process. The main aim of the Element is to provide critical insights into EMI implementation and the results obtained so far in diverse university contexts. After defining EMI and analyzing the rapid extension it has experienced, the Element tackles issues such as stakeholders' views on how EMI programs are being implemented, the impact of teaching and learning both content and language in a foreign language, translanguaging practices in English-medium lectures, and how assessment has hitherto been addressed. Each section aims to bring to light new avenues for research. The Element wraps up with a description of the many challenges ahead.

Keywords: EMI, higher education, stakeholders, teacher training, results

© David Lasagabaster 2022

ISBNs: 9781108829052 (PB), 9781108903493 (OC)
ISSNs: 2632-4415 (online), 2632-4407 (print)

Contents

1 Introduction

The current role of English as the main academic lingua franca is beyond any doubt. The epitome of this linguistic hegemony can be seen in the increasing number of universities the world over that are offering English-medium instruction (EMI) among their course options. The mushrooming of EMI is inextricably linked to universities' desire to attract international students, teaching staff, and researchers, to increase mobility, to augment revenue, to climb up education ranking systems, to improve English proficiency, and, last but not least, to enable graduate students to use English effectively in the workplace of the twenty-first century. At a time in which internationalization has become a mantra in the discourse of higher education institutions, EMI represents one of the most preeminent tools in university language policy in order to achieve the aforementioned internationalization-related objectives (Doiz, Lasagabaster & Sierra, 2013a; Kirkpatrick, 2011a; van der Walt, 2013). Altbach and Knight (2007) define internationalization as the policies and practices undertaken by academic systems and higher education institutions to tackle the global academic environment. Yet, this international drive is not something new, as it stems from these institutions' medieval origins in Europe and their desire to attract both faculty and students from diverse countries. The main difference with any previous period, however, has to do with its scale, as this torrent has never been seen before in history and its surge in the last two decades is unparalleled.

In this context, Englishization (the use of English in educational contexts where local languages were previously used) has become such a global trend that Macaro (2018: 300) considers that little can be done "to halt the express train of EMI." Chapple (2015: 1) has defined it as "a 'galloping' phenomenon now 'pandemic' in proportion," a quite telling expression in the current COVID-19 situation, while Block and Khan (2021: 7) put it down to a "resigned general sense of TINA (there is no alternative)." In fact, EMI programs can even be found in countries in which there has been very little foreign language teaching tradition, such as China, Italy, Japan, Saudi Arabia, or Spain. In China, for example, Hu and Lei (2014: 564) claim that "it is no exaggeration to say that English proficiency has become a most coveted form of cultural capital in Chinese society." Some authors (e.g. O'Dowd, 2018) have mentioned that it looks as if higher education institutions were willing to jump on the EMI bandwagon despite the fact that, strikingly, they show little commitment to delivering fully fledged programs. On many occasions, the willingness to appear on the EMI picture is much more determinant than the actual support that EMI stakeholders garner from their institutions. As a result of this situation, an influx of literature has appeared that examines the influence of EMI language policy (Darquennes, du Plessis & Soler, 2020; Wilkinson & Gabriëls, 2021) and that aims to ensure quality bilingual or multilingual practices at university level (Rubio-Alcalá & Coyle, 2021). It is important to note in this Introduction that, although EMI programs are immensely diverse, due to the succinct and dynamic nature of Cambridge Elements, some sections and topics are ineluctably concise because synthesizing is of the essence.

EMI entails different challenges that need to be faced, but perhaps of greatest import is that teaching staff need to deliver and students need to learn high-stakes content in an L2 (a second or additional language). But which contexts can be considered to be EMI? This acronym needs to be understood before we go any further.

2 Definition of EMI

Definitions are always narrow, constrained, and prone to criticism, and may even lead to more questions than answers. This is also the case with the term EMI, the definition of which has sparked debate (for a backdrop of terminological issues, see Macaro, 2018 and Pecorari & Halmström, 2018a). Nevertheless, and despite their inherent limitations and a lack of consensus among researchers, definitions help us to make sense of the world. With this in mind, EMI can be defined as "the use of the English language to teach academic subjects (other than English itself) in countries or jurisdictions where the first language of the majority of the population is not English" (Macaro et al., 2018: 37). This definition implies that countries included in the so-called inner circle (Australia, Canada, New Zealand, the United Kingdom, or the United States), wherein English is an official language, would be excluded from EMI.

The term EMI is habitually used together with other words and acronyms such as Englishization, CLIL (content and language integrated learning), ICLHE (integration of content and language in higher education), and EME (English-medium education), among others. Although these terms are often used interchangeably or authors prefer one over the others, in the following paragraphs I will briefly summarize the reasons why I have decided to keep using EMI.

Englishization is defined by Wilkinson and Gabriëls (2021) as the process through which English is gradually gaining ground in some particular domains (mainly education, politics, culture, and economics) in which another language was used before. In the domain of higher education, English clearly holds the upper hand and many aspects of academia (teaching –especially at master's level – publications, etc.) have switched to it, while the vernacular language loses not only space but also status. However, Englishization covers more aspects than just instruction – our reason for using it in this text – but its wider scope prevents us from using it as the main label for this Element. Moreover, according to Wilkinson and Gabriëls, it is an evaluative-descriptive term that may embody negative connotations for some of its users, whereas EMI remains more neutral.

In the case of the term CLIL, this is much more common at pre-university levels and refers to an approach with an explicit dual focus on language and content. Although the connections between CLIL and EMI are evident, the lack of integration between language and content on the part of EMI university lecturers has led many researchers to disregard the CLIL acronym and use the label EMI at tertiary level. Aguilar (2017) points out that content is the priority in EMI and, although incidental language learning is expected (Banegas & Manzur Busleimán, 2021), there are usually no clear-cut and explicit language objectives. Different research studies have borne this out (Macaro, 2018), as in EMI programs, language is not assessed and the collaboration of content and language lecturers is conspicuous by its absence (unlike in CLIL, where such collaboration is not only advised but actually fostered). In this vein, in their review of no less than 496 studies that used the acronym EMI, Pecorari and Halmström (2018a) observed that 87 percent of them were set in contexts of tertiary education, which confirms the close association of EMI with higher education.

Although the initialism ICLHE (integrating content and language in higher education) is also becoming commonplace in research studies undertaken in higher education, it can also be applied to languages other than English. In fact, I teach in a bilingual institution in which both Basque and Spanish are official languages, and thus ICLHE could refer, besides English, to either of them. Therefore, EMI is much more precise and defines an educational choice in which English is the medium of instruction.

Finally, Dafouz and Smit (2020) coined the term EMEMUS (English-medium education in multilingual university settings), or EME for short, and assert the following to defend the use of this term:

> EMEMUS is conceptually wider in the sense that it is inclusive of diverse research agendas, pedagogical approaches and of different types of education, comprising, for instance, online programmes and teacher pedagogical development. Furthermore, the concept is more transparent because it refers to "education," thus embracing both "instruction" and "learning" instead of prioritising one over the other. (3)

The acronym is clearly focused on the tertiary level (university) and acknowledges that English coexists with other languages on campus (multilingual), but what makes it truly distinctive is the inclusion of the word "education" to encompass both instruction and learning. Although EMEMUS is rapidly gaining ground, it is still not as popular as EMI.

When it comes to terminology, and especially when surrounded by these many different options, researchers should define from the very beginning what they mean. Thus, I have decided to stick to EMI because it is a widely used term that is deeply seated in the literature, as found by Pecorari and Halmström (2018a), as mentioned earlier. This is also the reason why, in this Element, I will not make reference to studies and authors that use EMI to refer to pre-university levels.

3 EMI at University Level

In this section, the factors that have contributed to the rapid spread of EMI will be considered, as well as its impact on the language ecology of the institutions concerned. In the specific case of EMI, language ecology refers to the study of how English interacts with the other languages and their environment, that is, the various social factors that surround any of the languages in contact. Language is a social practice that takes place in a social context, and therefore it cannot be considered in isolation.

3.1 The Spread of EMI

The main instigators of the Englishization of higher education have been politicians, educational institutions, and policymakers (Lanvers & Hultgren, 2018) in a top-down fashion easily recognizable in many contexts all over the world (Corrales, Rey, & Escamilla, 2016; Dearden, 2015). Therefore, EMI is sometimes not considered to be an approach but rather a political – and therefore a hierarchical – decision. South Korea is a very good case in point, as South Korean universities receive financial government support depending on the proportion of EMI courses offered. In this way, this economic incentive has become a powerful tool to foster interest in EMI among South Korean higher education institutions (Byun et al., 2011) and has helped to provoke an increase in the international student population (Kim, 2017). In a similar vein, in 2011 the Chinese Ministry of Education issued a directive in which universities were urged to offer 5–10 percent of undergraduate courses in English (or other foreign languages) in three years (Peng & Xie, 2021). The South Korean and Chinese cases bring to light that Asian countries adopting EMI are not constrained to those formerly colonized by English-speaking countries (e.g. Hong Kong, India, Malaysia, or Singapore), where EMI has been very popular for decades now, but that this trend is much wider in scope. As a result of this, many universities are not monolingual anymore and offer either whole programs, or at least some modules in – inevitably – English.

The impact of neoliberal global forces in the search for profit should also not be disregarded when talking about the spread of EMI, since English has become an indispensable part of the market, as it helps to make graduates more competitive and *marketable*. As Ryan (2018: 16) puts it, "EMI appears to reflect neoliberal market-oriented discourse that assumes a key role in using English to promote outward-looking, internationalisation perspectives." This neoliberal approach has undoubtedly helped EMI to blossom globally, since higher education has become a lucrative industry, the economic impact of which "contributes to global academic capitalism" (Gill & Kirkpatrick, 2013: 1–2). In this vein, universities also see EMI as a way to seize a portion of the major English-speaking countries' market share of international students and they tend to acknowledge it (more or less openly) in their language planning and policy. Kirkpatrick (2011b) highlights that Malaysian medical students are taking their degrees at Russian universities because the cost is 75 percent cheaper than that of a British or Australian university. He also points out that until very recently, the internationalization of Asian universities consisted mainly of students travelling to "western" countries to obtain degrees, which proved a highly profitable business for providing institutions while it meant both an economic and a brain drain for the sending countries. The implementation of EMI thus entails an attempt to attract international students while retaining local ones.

Language policy becomes a key element. Liddicoat (2018: 2) underscores that "the impact of internationalisation on the language planning of universities can be seen in all areas of academic work, in teaching and learning, in research and in administration." As a result of the preferential treatment given to English in many university contexts, it has been incorporated as an additional means of instruction alongside the national language(s). However, language policy is often hard to pinpoint at the micro level, that is, at the institutional level. In a very illustrative example, Marcos-García and Pavón (2018) scrutinized the web pages of seventy-six Spanish universities (fifty state and twenty-six private) and were surprised by the fact that only eighteen of them had an accessible document establishing their language policy. This is even more striking taking into account that all these higher education institutions had regularly increased the number of credits delivered in English on a yearly basis. This is a clear indication that top-down decisions are not always underpinned by clear-cut language policy documents, and that their visibility and accessibility leaves much to be desired.

Risager (2012: 112) distinguishes three main types of language policies when analyzing the introduction of English as a lingua franca in tertiary education:

(i) an English-only monolingual language policy in which other languages play second fiddle or none at all; (ii) a bilingual language policy in which English (maybe occasionally along with other international languages) goes hand in hand with the national language; and (iii) a trilingual language policy in which English is used together with the regional and the national languages (and maybe occasionally other international languages). The following sections will provide examples that dovetail with these three different types.

In terms of the different types of EMI programs found in the literature, Baker and Hüttner (2017) distinguish three main types: (i) student mobility programs in non-anglophone settings that attract students from a wide range of countries; (ii) internationalization-at-home programs to provide local students with EMI due to the impossibility of sending out all of them (from a theoretical standpoint, these programs incorporate intercultural perspectives while dealing with global issues and boosting participation in international activities); and (iii) Anglophone-context programs in which student bodies have become massively internationalized. Since, according to the definition provided earlier, this third type should not be included in EMI literature, I will not address it in the sections that follow. As for the first and the second types, they may also be merged, as many universities endeavor to attract both mobility and local students through EMI courses.

In the next few paragraphs, I will focus on the spread of EMI by continent. In the European context, the Erasmus exchange program and the Bologna Process were originally designed to boost student mobility programs and multilingual-ism among university stakeholders. However, reality has shown that English is becoming predominant in some specializations, especially in northern Europe, albeit not so much in southern countries. The Netherlands and the Nordic countries were trailblazers in using EMI in Europe, but its spread has nowadays reached even countries that in the past had little English as a foreign language learning tradition, such as Italy, Greece, and Spain (Doiz, Lasagabaster, & Sierra, 2013a). In a widely quoted work – because it is one of the few large-scale EMI studies – Wächter and Maiworm (2014) examined the presence of English-taught programs (ETPs) in Europe. Twenty-eight European countries participated in their survey but the authors only focused on ETPs that were 100-percent taught in English. Therefore, mixed programs taught both in the local language and English were excluded, despite the fact that in some contexts they are much more commonplace than ETPs. Strikingly, the survey revealed that ETPs had increased by 239 percent in just seven years (between 2007 and 2014) when the results were compared with those of a previous study by the same authors. However, ETPs were much more common in northern Europe than in the south, the geographical divide being quite remarkable. The number of students enrolled on ETPs varied considerably and ranged from a low 0.3 percent in Spain or 0.5 percent in Italy (both at the bottom of the proportion of students enrolled on ETPs) to 12.4 percent in Denmark or 4.4 percent in Sweden (both at the top of the ranking). Over the last few years, however, Denmark has been reducing EMI programs across different universities, whereas they are still growing in Sweden. Nonetheless, there are some common trends, such as the fact that they are more commonplace at master's and doctorate levels, and are more likely to proliferate in some disciplines (business and management, social sciences, and engineering and technology) than others (law or medicine at bachelor's level).

Disparity can even be found within the same country. In a survey carried out in Italy, Costa and Coleman (2013) reported that EMI was much more popular in universities in the north of the country (90 percent of them offering EMI courses) or the centre (87.5 percent) than in the south (only 22 percent). However, differences were also detected depending on the discipline, the growth of the courses being more common in some fields of knowledge than others.

According to Galloway, Kriukow, and Numajiri (2017), in Asia some country-specific studies have been completed but a large-scale study on the spread of EMI is still missing and "there is yet to be such a thorough investigation of this trend as in Europe" (9). However, the competition for international students in East Asia has exerted a knock-on effect and contributed to EMI being established in many universities. Taiwan is illustrative of this, as its government decided to boost EMI because its members were afraid of competition from neighboring countries. A program to promote international competitiveness was thus launched that included measures aimed at encouraging courses in English. Similar programs can be found in other Asian countries, although the language policies undertaken have varied considerably from country to country. For example, whereas South Korean universities aim to introduce EMI in all their existing programs, Japanese universities have gone for only a few 100-percent English-taught programs (Byun et al., 2011), and EMI "is still at an experimental stage in China, and has developed unevenly in different regions" (Zhang, 2017: 6–7).

In the Middle East, in countries such as the United Arab Emirates or Saudi Arabia, local universities are forging partnerships with universities from the United States and the United Kingdom to increase the presence of EMI in order to attract international students and investments. The so-called branch campus or satellite campus is becoming popular – that is, a university abroad that is part of a university located in an English-speaking country, the students of which get a highly regarded degree granted by a reputable English-speaking university.

This is an example of the internationalization-at-home programs mentioned earlier, as many of the students may never have been abroad. Although US universities are leading the way, UK, some continental European, and Australian universities are following suit and opening branch campuses throughout Asia. These can be found in Thailand, Vietnam, Singapore, India, or China, to name but a few countries (Altbach & Knight, 2007).

To my knowledge, EMI has not received much attention in Latin America and, in fact, the information about its expansion is very patchy. Authors nevertheless agree on pointing out that EMI is at its earliest stages in this part of the world (Martinez, 2016; Tejada-Sánchez & Molina-Naar, 2020), probably because top-down pressures have not been so unrelenting (Berry & Taylor, 2013). However, there is an increasing social awareness about the social and economic capital that English implies. This is stimulating the spread of EMI, to the extent that Tejada-Sánchez and Molina-Naar (2020: 364) conclude that "EMI is inevitable in this region." In their critical review of CLIL/EMI in Latin America between 2008 and 2018, Banegas, Poole, and Corrales (2020) conclude that most studies tend to be small-scale, usually carried out by teacher researchers focusing on their own practices. Although, as the authors claim, EMI is still in an embryonic state, they "envisage sustained expansion as a default approach for bilingual or English-medium education" (298). In a study focused on the largest Latin American country, Gimenez and colleagues (2018) gathered information from eighty-four Brazilian universities and 79 percent of them were already offering EMI, while a further 6 percent were planning to do so. More than 1,000 programs, courses, and activities were found, the largest percentage of them taking place at postgraduate level. This represented a significant increase with respect to the 50 percent of universities that offered EMI in a previous survey in 2016, just two years before. This growth could be attributed to the incentives provided by the Brazilian Ministry of Education to bolster internationalization. Defining the role of English in education has also become a priority for the Colombian government, while English has been positioned as a key factor of its internationalization strategy (Tejada-Sánchez & Molina-Naar, 2020). All these authors coincide in that lack of English proficiency is one of the main weaknesses of Latin American education systems, which is why hopes have been placed on the positive impact that EMI may have in this regard. However, they also warn that unequal power relations may limit EMI implementation to a handful of institutions.

Although Africa is the continent about which less information is readily available (Macaro et al., 2018), similar concerns to those in Latin America can be found in the literature. Excluding South Africa, this continent has the fewest cross-borders initiatives (Altbach & Knight, 2007). A number of branch campuses can be found in several countries (Egypt, Nigeria, Kenya, etc.), but it is really hard to find any additional information about EMI practices outside these international partnerships (Darquennes, du Plessis, & Soler, 2020).

In conclusion, variation and heterogeneity remain intrinsic features of EMI programs, but it is hard to challenge the widespread belief that EMI will carry on spreading and it is here to stay. International associations such as ICLHE (Integrating Content and Language in Higher Education; see https://iclhe.org/) or the launch of journals specifically focused on this field of research, such as the *Journal of English-Medium Instruction* (https://benjamins.com/catalog/jemi), are also conspicuous examples of the interest that EMI has raised among researchers. However, although in general university governing bodies' firm commitment to jump on the EMI bandwagon seems to be enough to avert any hurdle on the track, the decision to make English the language of instruction and scientific research has provoked controversy in contexts as diverse as the Arabian/Persian Gulf (Belhiah & Elhami, 2015), South Korea (Kim, 2017), the European Nordic countries (Kuteeva, Kaufhold, & Hynninen, 2020), or Italy (Pulcini & Campagna, 2015). Such controversy has been sparked by the belief that EMI may have a detrimental effect on higher education institutions' multilingualism and language ecology, our next topic of interest.

3.2 EMI and Multilingualism

One of the most controversial issues relating to the spread of EMI lies in universities' endeavors to foster multilingualism, which may be hampered by English overshadowing the other national and international languages in contact. It is in this context that the concept of "language ecology" comes to the fore (see Haugen, 1971), which can be defined as the study of how languages interact with each other and with the surrounding social factors in a given context, and how their use and status can be preserved. In this way, ecology becomes a metaphor from biology that is used in educational linguistics, and language management and planning at tertiary level.

In this regard, two main schools of thought can be distinguished. On the one hand, authors such as Phillipson (2006) warn against the perils associated with the hegemony of major English-speaking countries (native speakers being in an advantageous position) and the social inequalities exacerbated by EMI (high English proficiency being realistically reachable only by students belonging to privileged social classes). These fears led him to coin the well-known term "linguistic imperialism," a concept that describes the imposition of an imperial power's language policy on third parties who cannot face the pressure exerted by global forces to push Englishization. The publication of research results could be a good example of this hegemony. Nowadays, researchers are required to publish in indexed journals that may lead to high citation scores (the higher the number of citations, the more influential a researcher becomes), and journal rankings have privileged research completed in English. Since English is the language of such journals, the language choice is far from being open and the linguistic pressure exerted by this policy can be clearly seen in the small share of publications in languages other than English. Some research areas such as humanities and social sciences may be more prone to find this language/science policy problematic, as their work is deeply embedded in their specific cultural setting, and research output in English may not be viable. Since the bulk of scientific publication is written in English, EMI is believed to cater for students' need to be able to read specialized language in their specific academic fields with ease. Haberland (2014) argues that the imposition of English has been facilitated not only by the decisions made by administrators and the acceptance by those who have to put it into practice, but also by language ideologies (that is, conceptualizations about languages influenced by political and economic interests) that support that EMI is possible. In fact, this situation has brought about linguistic tensions surrounding the issue of domain loss of the local languages in the European Nordic countries, particularly in the sciences, since English has a higher status than the local languages (Kuteeva, Kaufhold, & Hynninen, 2020). As a result of this, language policies have stirred heated debates in the Nordic context due to the increasing presence of English not only at university level but also in the wider social sphere, which has led to a certain sense of language domination and to the belief that universities' language ecology may be jeopardized.

On the other hand, university authorities and some researchers strongly believe that EMI will help to pave the way to ecologically balanced multilingual institutions, as the local and the global language can coexist and even strengthen each other. Since Englishization is inextricably intertwined with identity, if the local cultural identity is underpinned and the stakeholders are given voice, this glocal (global and local) perspective will benefit universities and will bolster the internationalization process (Lasagabaster, 2021b). Other scholars such as Van Parijs (2011) support a more pragmatic vision and highlight the usefulness of English as a translingual communication tool. Although multilingualism and internationalization more often than not become euphemistic terms to refer to English (Saarinen, 2012), in many higher education institutions local languages are not being upstaged by English because they are strongly associated with identity and utility. This was confirmed by Vila and Bretxa (2015), who examined the language policies of medium-sized languages at university level. The authors define medium-sized languages as "all those placed between the biggest and the smallest languages" (4) and include Danish, Czech, Finnish, Swedish in Finland, Hebrew, and Afrikaans in their volume. The authors conclude that these languages are far from disappearing from the academic world and claim that, as long as they are supported by political, social, and academic institutions and remain solidly established on all the rungs of the educational ladder, their position will not be threatened by English and EMI.

At any rate, there is agreement that Englishization can have both positive and negative effects. The conviction that English is the key to internationalization is thoroughly documented in many countries in diverse continents, and, consequently, many universities cannot escape the use of English as means of instruction (van der Walt, 2013). In Europe, transnational institutions have committedly fostered the Bologna Process to create a single education and research area with the purported objective of boosting the recognition of academic qualifications, mobility programs, employability, and, last but not least, multilingualism. However, the increasing presence of English may dispossess the other languages (national language, co-official languages, and other foreign languages). Some voices have claimed that the Bologna Process has actually undermined the goal of multilingualism by leaving very little space, if any, for other foreign languages (Costa & Coleman, 2013). This is so even in southern European universities, despite the fact that English does not play such a paramount role as in Nordic countries and EMI only occurs in selected faculties. Thus, Italian teaching staff declare that they are concerned about Italian losing prominence in some areas of knowledge (Broggini & Costa, 2017), and it is feared that the Italian language and culture may be impoverished if EMI is uncritically embraced (Motta, 2017). This ties in with the "paradox of internationalization," coined by Haberland and Preisler (2015), according to which the more languages lecturers and students speak, the more likely they will adopt English as the language of communication.

But some institutions have managed to surf the English-only effect and have been able to actually foster multilingualism. A particularly interesting case is that of officially bilingual universities where English is promoted as an L3 (third language) on EMI courses. This is the case of universities with agendas that aim to promote a minority or minoritized language that coexists with the national language, such as Basque/Catalan/Galician with Spanish in Spain, Russian with Kazakh in Kazakhstan, Belarusian and Russian in Belarus, Swedish with Finnish in Finland, Bantu languages with Afrikaans in South Africa, Arabic with Hebrew in Israel, or Frisian with Dutch in the Netherlands. These universities are obliged to invest more resources than other monolingual institutions because in their case internationalization involves a truly multilingual situation wherein the international languages of communication (the national and English) coexist with the languages of identity (the national and/or the minoritized language). This multilingual context sometimes generates tensions depending on the linguistic standpoint of the different stakeholders, but trilingualism has been institutionalized and efforts have been made to strike a balance between small languages and English. The former provide a sense of identity and retain a strong symbolic value, whereas the latter opens doors in the international arena. Although the importance of EMI is taken for granted, it is counterbalanced with the paramount role that the minority and the national languages play when it comes to authentic immersion into the culture and life of the host institution and society, and the value attached to multilingualism as linguistic, cultural, and symbolic capital.

In this vein, the *Plan of Action for Multilingualism* passed at Pompeu Fabra University in Catalonia in 2007 is worth mentioning because it is an example of how multilingualism can be boosted at tertiary level. This plan is based on four principles:

(i) The need to strengthen and increase the presence of Catalan in all spheres of activity.

(ii) The status of English as a working language.

(iii) The establishment of the principle of "linguistic security" for both lecturers and students. To this effect, lecturers have to make public the language in which their classes will be held and will have to stick to this language, whereas students will be assured the right to use the language they wish from the two official languages of Catalonia (Catalan and Spanish) and English. This will guarantee the possibility of using the three languages within the university community.

(iv) The implementation of a protocol for managing multilingualism in the classroom, which will foster the coexistence and interaction of languages while safeguarding the linguistic rights and obligations of all parties involved.

This language policy is the foundation to progress toward functional multilingualism as the three languages are used and can be used in the institutional, academic, and administrative spheres. To achieve this aim, both lecturers and students should possess productive knowledge in at least one of the three languages and receptive knowledge of the two other languages, so that everyone has the opportunity to use the language they feel most comfortable with. The "linguistic security" principle is thus vital, since all academic activities and materials (including exams) must be conducted and given in the language advertised before the start of each course and made public with sufficient notice (that is, English in EMI courses), but students will be free to use any of the three languages. In this way, the plan helps "to strike a balance between necessary internationalization and an irrevocable preservation of the local language in university teaching" (Pompeu Fabra University 2007: 21).

In the same vein, the policy document entitled *More Parallel, Please* and published by the Nordic Council of Ministers (Gregersen et al., 2018) sets out eleven recommendations on the parallel use of local and international languages in the Nordic Region. The recommendations are the following:

(i)   Every university should have a language policy.

(ii) Every university should have a language policy committee.

(iii) Every university should have a language centre.

(iv) Staff recruited abroad should be offered courses in the teaching language, common speech, and language for special purposes.

(v)   Various categories of students should be offered language courses, following needs analyses.

(vi) Lecturers and researchers should be offered language courses, following needs analyses.

(vii) Universities should choose their teaching languages based on the principles of parallel language use and the "international classroom."

(viii) University language policies should also cover the language used in the administration.

(ix) The universities should monitor and regularly reassess the choice of language for publications.

(x)   University language policies should also cover the language used in dissemination of knowledge, outreach, and external communication activities.

(xi) Language policies should include developing digital language-support resources at every university.

These policies are two examples of how universities can succeed in showing minority and local language speakers that there is an institutional commitment to protecting their linguistic rights, which will help stop EMI being seen as a Trojan horse undermining progress made so far in revitalizing their minoritized language and/or maintaining the local language. This will undoubtedly pave the way toward actual multilingualism in these universities (more on this in Section 5.3).

4 Stakeholders' Views

The Englishization of higher education has bolstered heated debates in both the more limited academic sphere and wider public spheres. Researchers have shown great interest in gathering information about stakeholders' opinions regarding EMI implementation, which is why there is extensive research, based on self-reporting data, exploring attitudes toward EMI and the perceived challenges and benefits. Questionnaires and/or interviews have been the most frequent instruments used to gather data. In the following sections, the views of lecturers, students, and administration personnel will be examined, which will lead us to some final reflections on stakeholders' stances regarding EMI.

4.1 Lecturers' Views

Lecturers' beliefs and opinions have been widely scrutinized. Broadly speaking, lecturers are very positive about introducing EMI programs and see it as a natural part of the process of internationalizing universities. The advantages lecturers draw from EMI usually revolve around easier access to materials in English, using specialized vocabulary in English, the possibility of speaking English in authentic communicative situations while building language confidence, attracting more international students, who contribute to making classes more international, and the positive impact of the EMI experience on the internationalization process in general (e.g. increased participation in mobility programs) and in the institution's position in university rankings in particular (Corrales, Rey, & Escamilla, 2016; Doiz, Lasagabaster, & Sierra, 2013; Guarda & Helm, 2017a; Henriksen, Holmen, & Kling, 2019). That said, differences between disciplines have been found (Kuteeva & Airey, 2014).

However, the aforementioned studies recurrently reveal that English language competence appears as the main stumbling block, to the extent that it may negatively affect the teaching approach and teaching strategies. In fact, in many EMI contexts, one of the main characteristics is that lectures are far from being dialogic and are based on long monologues in which interaction is conspicuous by its absence, and whenever it takes place, it is usually in the form of short exchanges with a few words or short sentences (Doiz & Lasagabaster, 2021).

Lecturers on EMI courses tend to feel insecure due to their inability to tackle language problems. They also complain about the additional effort and extra time that goes into preparing their lessons, the greater complexity of getting ideas and concepts across when compared with teaching in their first language (L1) (see Thøgersen & Airey, 2011), and the tiredness that using a foreign language produces. In Japan, it has been estimated that it takes EMI lecturers four to five times more effort to teach in English than in Japanese (Bradford, 2019). All these factors negatively affect their self-confidence. They also appear concerned about their students' language command (Bradford, 2019; Tejada-Sánchez & Molina-Naar, 2020), which forces them to frequently check their understanding of the topic. Yet, they affirm that their main goal is to communicate in English and that students should not be afraid of making mistakes, as the vast majority of EMI lecturers do not take language mistakes into account, nor is their evaluation conditioned by the number of mistakes.

Lecturers on EMI courses see themselves as instructors who teach content in English but not the English language itself, and this is a finding recurrent in the literature irrespective of the country. Not only do EMI content lecturers show a clear tendency to align themselves with their respective academic disciplines, but they also firmly reject the role of language lecturers and present themselves as "lecturers who just happen to teach some of their subjects in English" (Block, 2021: 402). In South Korea, Kim, Kim, and Kweon (2018) investigated the attitudes of teaching staff at three universities, and the participants reported the benefits of EMI as far as internationalizing the university was concerned, but they also underscored that content learning should be their primary aim, as they were content specialists who had no training in language teaching. Many researchers have come across very similar findings in Europe in university contexts as diverse as Italy (Costa, 2012), Spain (Aguilar, 2017), or Sweden (Airey, 2012). Curiously enough, both quantitative (Doiz and Lasagabaster, 2021) and qualitative (Block, 2021) approaches seem to indicate that those who are most competent and confident about their English turn out to be the lecturers who shun the idea of being English language teachers.

One of the few studies (Dafouz, Hüttner, & Smit, 2016) that garnered lecturers' viewpoints from different European contexts (Austria, Finland, Spain, and the United Kingdom) concluded that the integration of content and language is viewed as a central and complex concern, shared by all eighteen interviewees. Three main differences were mentioned by the participants when L1 medium of instruction and EMI were compared: (1) EMI demands increased preparation time; (2) students find learning more difficult due to mainly language-related issues, including both general proficiency and subject-specific language; and (3) lecturers' practices aim to reduce such difficulties in EMI, despite finding the integration of content and language very complex. The strategies used by EMI lecturers included reducing the delivery speech, providing additional language support, offering visual support, explaining unknown words (preemptive language-related episodes being recurrently found also by Doiz and Lasagabaster [2021]), avoiding ambiguities (especially in exam situations), or focusing on numerical information while downplaying the role of language.

Lecturers are also subject to the tensions over native-like and non-native–like English ideologies, but they usually go for English as a lingua franca practices (that is, any use of English among speakers of different first languages), while they value student comprehension over accuracy (Doiz & Lasagabaster, 2018; Kuteeva, Kaufhold, & Hynninen, 2020; Murata, 2019). This is closely linked to lecturers' great concern regarding pronunciation, an issue that has been repeatedly put under the spotlight in Spanish-speaking contexts such as Spain (Doiz, Lasagabaster, & Pavón, 2019) and Mexico (Núñez Asomoza, 2015). Lecturers often mention that they find the pronunciation of technical vocabulary particularly challenging (the word "sovereignty" in history being a very good case in point), to the extent that many of them perceive pronunciation problems as one of the most demanding questions to be resolved in their lectures. However, they also declare that their objective is "to surpass the level of intelligibility, having pronunciation as an ally to make concepts and ideas intelligible and not as a source of frustration in an unrealistic attempt to achieve native-like accuracy" (Doiz, Lasagabaster, & Pavón, 2019: 172).

Another issue that concerns the EMI faculty has to do with teaching large classes of students, because this impedes lecturers from both implementing a more student-centered approach in their teaching and interacting with students whose language proficiency may vary considerably as a result of the great diversity of language proficiencies found in such large classes (Guarda & Helm, 2017a). Selection criteria based on English proficiency is disregarded in many universities on the grounds that principles of equality in education should prevail, which is why any student with an interest can enroll on EMI courses without their command of English being assessed. The side-effect of this policy is that lecturers may have to teach groups whose English skills differ sharply, and this complicates their teaching.

Last but not least, EMI practitioners realize that intercultural competence has become very important as they have to face student bodies that are increasingly diverse. In some universities, classes have shifted from very homogeneous student bodies, in which the vast majority of students, if not all, shared the same L1 and culture, to student bodies in which a rich variety of L1 and cultures coexist.

4.2 Students' Perceptions

In general terms, students also appear to be favorably disposed toward EMI and the reasons in support of their positive stance tend to match those mentioned by their lecturers, although students also mention negative aspects, as we will see in this section. In addition, students are especially positive because it is seen as a tool that will open new possibilities in their professional or academic career (Arkim & Osam, 2015). In fact, undergraduates find EMI in higher education an interesting option as it increases their symbolic and economic capital, as also noted by Doiz, Costa, Lasagabaster, and Mariotti (2019), Valcke and Wilkinson (2017), and Wächter and Maiworm (2014), to mention but a few.

Although generalizations are hard to make, EMI students tend to underscore that the use of English as means of instruction increases the complexity of the learning process. Language proficiency plays a very important role in this matter, as those who are more proficient face fewer difficulties and those with less command are more worried. However, EMI does not appear to negatively affect either learning outcomes or course satisfaction, although some studies have found that students would prefer an implementation that would move from less to more complex subject matter (Arnó-Maciá & Aguilar-Pérez, 2021).

As far as English learning is concerned, they tend to believe that EMI has a very positive impact on the development of the four language skills, even in those contexts in which students' language proficiency is low (Belhiah & Elhami, 2015). However, they also acknowledge some linguistic limitations. Students usually regard vocabulary, writing, and speaking as the most challenging areas of EMI. It is not surprising that disciplinary vocabulary is often reported to be a major hurdle for students, as the lack of vocabulary knowledge impedes their comprehension of lectures and texts (Evans & Morrison, 2011a). In speaking, their main concerns have to do with oral presentations and their participation in discussions. In writing, they find particularly difficult the organization of essays and the use of appropriate academic style (Kamasak, Hasan, & Rose, 2021), as they are not used to writing extended texts in English. Finally, they also feel vulnerable because of the difficulties they encounter with English pronunciation, which many undergraduates find really challenging. Therefore, special attention should be paid to productive skills and subject-specific vocabulary. In fact, when undergraduates are directly asked in what linguistic abilities they would like to receive language support, they tend to single out those related to oral and written production (Doiz et al., 2019).

These results make it difficult to grasp why students' English competence is usually taken for granted by higher education institutions' governing bodies, since studies recurrently indicate that this is an issue to which heed must be paid. Even in the Nordic countries, whose students always achieve top positions in surveys on English competence, undergraduates find difficulties when tackling academic English. This is due to the fact that the linguistic resources they acquire extramurally or at grassroots level (the social presence of English is large: for example, films and TV series are not dubbed) differ considerably from the academic English they have to face in EMI courses. As a result, they often struggle with the discipline-specific language. The EMI experience at university level makes them realize the problems that academic English poses for them and that there is a mismatch between the English they acquire prior to entering university and what is required in EMI.

In any case, the connections between students' self-assessment and their actual academic behavior are not always straightforward. Tatzl and Messnarz (2013) found a weak correlation between students' self-assessment of their problem-solving skills in physics and their measured test results, with an insignificant correlation coefficient of 15 percent. But the correlation between self-assessment of English language skills and test results was even weaker (a correlation coefficient of 9 percent, once again insignificant). Most students therefore overestimated both their problem-solving and English skills. These results tally with those obtained by Hernández-Nanclares and Jiménez-Muñoz (2017), who also observed that students' perception of their language production was richer, more varied, and accurate than their real performance actually evidenced. However, the results obtained by Joe and Lee (2013) run in the opposite direction, as the mismatch between students' perceived lecture comprehension and their actual performance proved: the negative correlation showed that their content knowledge did actually increase over the EMI course despite students showing dissatisfaction with it.

It is interesting to note that students' perceptions seem to vary depending on the continent under scrutiny. Thus, students enrolled in EMI programs in European institutions are generally more positive than those enrolled in EMI programs in Asian contexts, whose perceived lower English proficiency seems to make them harbor more unfavorable attitudes, as attested in different studies in China (Hu & Wu, 2020), Euro-Asian Turkey (Arkim & Osam, 2015), the Gulf (Belhiah & Elhami, 2015), Hong Kong (Evans & Morrison, 2011b), or South Korea (Kim & Yoon, 2018). Kim (2017) reports on one of the most striking outcomes to be found in EMI literature, resulting from the low English proficiency and the highly competitive environment of some Asian universities. In 2011, four South Korean undergraduates committed suicide in one of the country's most reputed universities, the rigid EMI policy implementation being partly held responsible for the students' deaths. This is obviously an extreme case, but it reflects how challenging EMI may turn out to be in some particular contexts.

Students also claim that the transmission style of teaching reigns supreme and they are reluctant to participate in class mainly due to three key reasons (Evans & Morrison, 2011b: 153): (1) discomfort at speaking before their peers; (2) lack of confidence in their English; and (3) unfamiliarity with the topic. Asian students are considered to be less interactive "than those from the Western educational systems" (Kim, 2017: 60), but in EMI classes their degree of interaction has been observed to be even lower. Students also express concern about those instances in which EMI is compulsory, as it puts too much pressure on both lecturers and students. The attitudes of students on these courses are not as positive as those in optional programs (Corrales, Rey, & Escamilla, 2016; Kim, 2017). Japanese EMI students enrolled in programs completely taught in English have also complained about the few opportunities to exchange opinions in large-class lectures, although this concern was lower on those programs in which only a few subjects were delivered in English, which indicates once again that language proficiency is a key issue (Konakahara, Murata, & Iino, 2019).

Studies have also analyzed ideologies regarding native language. Although native varieties are still deeply seated in students' conceptualization of language, they do not all enjoy the same status. Thus, native speakers of British or American English are more highly regarded than speakers of English as a lingua franca (ELF), but ELF speakers have more status than speakers of postcolonial varieties, despite these being native varieties (Kuteeva, 2020). In any case, students rate EMI lecturers' English proficiency above their being native English speakers. Other factors are deemed more important, such as EMI lecturers' familiarity with the students' local language and culture, their ability to simulate an international learning experience, or their display of effective teaching pedagogies as regards both content and language (Inbar-Lourie & Donitsa-Schmidt, 2020). In sum, the traits of the desired EMI practitioner extend far beyond the boundaries of nativeness, a concept that seems to be in the process of becoming old-fashioned for most students, although this is not always the case for governing bodies (Kim, 2017).

4.3 Administration Personnel's Opinions

Despite the fact that at most universities an international student's first contact is with a member of the administrative staff, there has been little research regarding these important members of the community.

By analyzing EMI from the perspectives of all those involved, we can learn more about its impact and inherent complexity. Unlike lecturers and students, the administrative team that facilitates the smooth functioning of universities work outside the classroom. This may be the reason why little research has been carried out concerning their feelings, attitudes, opinions, and role in EMI programs. However, administrative staff "are fundamental to the managing of any innovative policy and whose perspectives need to be considered" (Llurda, Cots, & Armengol, 2014: 390). The few studies available (Doiz, Lasagabaster, & Sierra, 2013) reveal that they are clearly in favor of EMI because of its positive impact on academic mobility, study abroad opportunities, students' career prospects, and, last but not least, the improvement of English proficiency it entails. Administration personnel usually show enthusiasm toward a multilingual university, which in their opinion should offer courses in different languages in addition to the official one(s).

To my knowledge, there is only one study (Doiz, Lasagabaster, & Sierra, 2014) that has actually measured and compared the support of lecturers, students, and administration personnel regarding EMI. It revealed that administrative staff were the most positive group regarding all the items included in the questionnaire, followed by the teaching staff and then the students. It is worth noting that the administration personnel were very favorable toward the presence of English at university, the need to teach nonlanguage modules in English, and the requirement for students to take a few modules in English and to be competent in English by the end of their studies.

Nonetheless, administrative staff are skeptical about whether students who have finished secondary education are sufficiently proficient in English to handle EMI courses at university, while they also bemoan and acknowledge their own failings in English. Similar results have been found in Latin America (Tejada-Sánchez & Molina-Naar, 2020), where administrators also appeared concerned about students' level of English.

The important role of the administrative staff was also emphasized by Ackerley, Guarda, and Helm (2017) during their focus on EMI at the University of Padova in Italy. This is one of the few volumes in which the editors gathered information from the three university bodies, by first focusing on the macro contexts of EMI in Europe and Italy, then devoting the bulk of the chapters to the micro context of their university. The language centre and the administrative staff (an international relations officer and a student services officer) were given a voice to reflect on and express the changes that EMI had brought about for them. The participants underscored that English competence is vital, but not enough, since intercultural competences are gaining ground in an ever more multilingual and multicultural university context. In fact, the international relations officer shared her feeling that European universities are shifting their concern from English language training to a more comprehensive training aimed at developing an intercultural mindset. The student services officer concluded by pointing out the profound impact that the higher degree of internationalization was having on their daily activities to accommodate the needs of both international and domestic students who graduate after having participated in EMI courses (e.g. the requirement to translate certificates and diploma supplements).

At the university of Vaasa in Finland, Järlström and colleagues (2020) found that a high percentage of the university services staff considered that their English command was at an excellent or good level: 75 percent of them in the case of productive language skills and 83 percent when it came to receptive skills. However, their linguistic problems strikingly had to do more with the two local languages (Finnish and Swedish) than English. In fact, while English skills were regarded as being at a high level by all groups, the same did not apply to their self-evaluation of Swedish (310). The university services staff found the translation work especially challenging (described as time-consuming) and affirmed that not all information could be translated into English on the university's website. As was the case in the study by Ackerley, Guarda, and Helm (2017), translation often becomes an issue in connection with higher education institutions' internationalization and the spread of EMI.

4.4 Final Remarks

Broadly speaking, Phillipson's (2006) and others' negative views of the Englishization process are not shared by the different university bodies, as they tend to harbor largely positive attitudes toward EMI, although they are also well aware of the challenges that need to be confronted. In an attempt to summarize the main findings, it could be said that stakeholders perceive EMI as a means to increase mobility, access to knowledge, and employability. Moreover, both lecturers and students tend to have the impressionistic feeling that through EMI their English improves (especially subject-specific English) without having any significant detrimental effect on content learning (Arnó-Maciá & Aguilar-Pérez, 2021).

However, there are important differences between university settings, depending on the way EMI has been implemented. In many contexts, the three university bodies (lecturers, students, and administration personnel) value EMI highly, but they all bemoan their lack of linguistic skills, a limitation that stems from the minor importance historically attached to foreign language learning in some countries. Therefore, all university bodies share the linguistic deficit view. Due to this shortcoming, EMI programs have only recently been implemented in many contexts, whereas in other contexts, such as the Netherlands or the Nordic countries, where foreign language learning has traditionally been fostered, EMI is more firmly established. The key issue is then not EMI per se, but rather how it is set in motion, as in those settings where it has not been properly implemented, it has negatively impacted on participants' attitudes, motivation, degree of satisfaction, and commitment. Stakeholders of EMI are mainly critical about the lack of support received from university authorities and demand more tailor-made courses, economic underpinnings, and human investment. However, they also acknowledge that EMI is a recent trend in most universities and will need time to settle in (Doiz, Lasagabaster, & Sierra, 2013b).

Differences have also been observed between EMI lecturers and students. Whereas lecturers are more focused on content, students are also interested in language learning and show a strong desire to use English, especially those enrolled on fully English-taught programs (Konakahara, Murata, & Iino, 2019). In this vein, Doiz and Lasagabaster (2018) observed that EMI students had incorporated English into their lives in a more natural way than their lecturers, for whom English did not come as naturally in their private lives (although it did in the work sphere). Thus, students had a more holistic English imagined community in mind that facilitated their contemplating their lives "outside university and diverse social spheres in English" (675). Other differences have also been found concerning language issues, such as lecturers being more concerned about their limited lexical resources in English, whereas students do not find this so frustrating as they directly look up unknown words in the dictionary or ask the lecturer for an explanation (Lasagabaster, 2021a).

Both lecturers and students coincide in highlighting that content lecturers should not assume the language lecturer role that researchers often assign to them (Block, 2021: Lasagabaster, 2021a), which is why, in their shared view, language issues should play an ancillary role in EMI lecturers' duties. This is a reflection of what Block (2021: 403) labels as "the delimiting effects of a disciplinary identity," as instructors identify themselves with their specialization but turn down any attempt to include an EFL gaze in their teaching. However, it is worth remembering that, despite the fact that EMI lecturers clearly favor content over language, research evidence reveals that language-related episodes do happen in their classes (Lasagabaster & Doiz, 2021). Airey (2012: 64) claims, and rightly so, that "from a disciplinary discourse perspective, all university courses can be said to involve content and language integrated learning (CLIL) even in monolingual settings," and therefore, all EMI lecturers are language teachers, whether they like it or not. This would lead us to what Lin (2016) describes as the "2-in-1" teacher, that is, a teacher who has both the awareness and capacity to perform the dual roles of content teacher and language teacher and can thus integrate content teaching with language teaching.

Similarly, both groups also coincide in finding reading and listening less problematic than speaking and writing. Although pronunciation is often mentioned as a source of insecurities, stakeholders also underscore that the international English they use in class helps them to overcome comprehensibility and intelligibility barriers. Thus, this ELF approach seems helpful to face the oral challenges that both lecturers and students come across in EMI (Doiz & Lasagabaster, 2018; Murata, 2019). This seems to confirm Kuteeva's (2020) assertion that ELF research should strive to identify the communicative strategies required for ensuring understanding among EMI stakeholders.

Administrative staff, although not directly involved in EMI but clearly affected by an increasingly more international university, usually hold very positive attitudes toward its implementation, although their lack of language competence becomes once again their main concern in many settings. The lack of attention paid to this university body should be remedied in future investigations.

Last but not least, I would like to refer to a comparative study of ten European universities in which Orduna-Nocito and Sánchez-García (2021) identified the misalignment between top-down internationalization policies and EMI beliefs and practices. In particular, the authors suggest that: (i) from a policy perspective, more effort should be put into disseminating EMI policies and reaching all stakeholders; (ii) from a pedagogical perspective, training should be more solid and varied and extended also to students; and (iii) from a linguistic perspective, English should not be considered as a mere communicative tool and discipline-specific epistemology should not be overlooked. These measures would contribute to make top-down and bottom-up perspectives meet and, consequently, to strengthen EMI programs. As suggested by the authors, future research should try to unearth the existing gaps between internationalization policies and EMI classroom realities, as well as the possible misalignments that can exist between the three university bodies. Only by getting to know how EMI is perceived by the whole university community will programs be able to make up for the weaknesses detected.

5 Impact of EMI on Teaching

There is no doubt that teaching in a foreign language exerts an influence on teaching practices. The first question that needs to be brought to the table is whether EMI lecturers are pedagogically prepared to face the EMI challenge. This is closely linked to team teaching and professional development, because team teaching (the collaboration of language and content lecturers) could help to integrate content and language learning objectives, whereas EMI lecturer professional development should be aimed at improving lecturers' pedagogical training. A second question that immediately comes to mind is whether EMI lecturers should allow the use of students' L1 in their classes or whether an English-only approach should prevail. These are the issues to be analyzed in this section.

5.1 Are Lecturers Pedagogically Prepared to Teach EMI Courses?

This question has hardly been tackled in many higher education institutions. The belief that the EMI boat could not be missed has led decision makers to implement EMI courses without proper consideration of the needs that have to be catered for. In fact, the lack of teaching training opportunities is rather widespread. Wächter and Maiworm (2014) undertook a survey in twenty-eight European countries and observed that, although English competence was often a key criterion when it came to recruiting lecturers, only a third of the more than 1,100 program directors answered positively to the question of whether their institutions offered courses aimed at addressing their lecturers' needs.

The results obtained by O'Dowd (2018) in a survey carried out among seventy European universities also revealed that 30 percent of the universities did not provide any form of teacher training, whereas 35 percent focused only on communication skills and did not consider any methodological course. Very similar findings were recorded by Sahan and colleagues (2021) in a recent survey that encompassed fifty-two countries around the world on the Official Development Assistance (ODA) list, as professional development opportunities were limited and focused mainly on improving university lecturers' general English competence rather than on developing the skills needed to teach academic content in English. It is worth pointing out that the question of pedagogical preparation of lecturers goes beyond EMI and also applies to teaching in the local language(s), as such training has been considered non-essential in many university contexts.

As for the required level of English proficiency, O'Dowd (2018) found that the range was very wide and some universities enabled their EMI lecturers to deliver their courses with a B2 certificate (European framework of reference for languages), while others were much more demanding and required a C2 certificate. Whereas some universities and EMI experts (Drljača Margić & Vodopija-Krstanović, 2018; Henriksen, Holmen, & Kling, 2019) consider that a B2 certificate is not adequate to teach complex contents at tertiary level, some Spanish universities accept it as sufficient proof of English language competence (Lasagabaster, 2022). In fact, one of the persons in charge of the accreditation of lecturers at a Spanish university informed me (personal communication) that they use a general English proficiency test in a reduced version that only measures listening and reading skills, with productive skills not considered. The exclusion of productive skills is due to purely economic reasons, as there is no budget to also assess them (this is the most complex and expensive part of exam). This lack of funding is a constant source of problems at some universities. Other universities have designed and developed their own instruments to assess their lecturers' English proficiency (see Dimova & Kling, 2018, or Dubow & Gundermann, 2017), their main disadvantage being that they are not recognized by other universities. At a time when the achievements of the European higher education area are often celebrated (especially when it comes to making education systems more compatible while strengthening quality assurance mechanisms), this lack of a common policy regarding teacher qualification is remarkable. In the Asian context, Galloway, Kriukow, and Numajiri (2017) also found varying levels of language proficiency requirement in Chinese and Japanese universities, which seems to indicate that this issue is universal, as linguistic requirements tend to be university-specific.

English competence has been the main concern for many stakeholders, as seen in Section 4. Dang and colleagues (2021) analyzed EMI from a global perspective to later focus on the Chinese context and observed that, both at the macro level and the meso level, English proficiency was one of EMI lecturers' main concerns. Helm and Guarda (2015) and Doiz, Lasagabaster, and Pavón (2019) gathered EMI lecturers' worries and observed that spoken fluency and informal interaction skills were the main concerns in all academic disciplines. This had an impact on their teaching because they acknowledged that on some occasions they tended to avoid particular conversational situations, which prevented them from building rapport with their students.

According to researchers (Bradford, 2019; Sánchez-Pérez, 2020; Werther, Denver, Jensen, & Mees, 2014), however, not only English proficiency but also pedagogical quality and intercultural communication become key factors when it comes to implementing cogent EMI programs. Thus, several authors suggest that teaching methodology should come under the spotlight, as there is an urgent need to move from the mainly monologic and little interactive EMI classroom to a more student-centered approach (Rose, 2021; Wilkinson, 2013). EMI classroom observation has proven that student–teacher interaction is conspicuous by its absence (Doiz & Lasagabaster, 2021; Macaro, 2018), which entails considerable risks because students are not given the opportunity to express their ideas in English. In fact, most of the time, their participation is constrained to short phrases and even to single words, while studies have shown that EMI courses are less interactive than those conducted in the lecturer's and the students' L1 (Airey, 2012). This is a key issue because interaction helps to develop students' cognitive abilities through exchanges with either the lecturer and/or peers. This sociocultural approach to education has led researchers to look into classroom talk, as learning is largely a social process the basis of which lies in interacting with other people. Surprisingly, although seminars with a more limited number of students that could foster a higher degree of interaction – in contrast to the interactional constraints imposed by larger classes – are habitual at some universities, there appears to be hardly any research on such settings (Macaro, 2018).

When analyzing interaction, the crucial role questions play in meaning-making and understanding needs greater attention. University lecturers can help to scaffold their students' learning by means of questions, but in many university settings students are unwilling to participate. In fact, the few studies available at university level have unearthed students' reluctance to ask questions due to their linguistic limitations in English (Engin, 2017), to the extent that they avoid asking questions in front of the whole class and prefer to ask the lecturer privately during breaks (Tsou, 2017). In an interesting study that compared questioning in EMI and in L1 classes in Swedish (Airey, 2009), students realized that they asked fewer questions in EMI after watching video recordings of their classes. This means that even in a country where undergraduates are expected to have a higher command of English than in many other settings, EMI exacerbates students' reluctance to pose questions.

In one of the scarce studies that has analyzed university lecturers' questions in depth, Sánchez-García (2020) observed that the number of questions was largely similar in the case of two business administration lecturers' practices in Spanish (L1) and EMI lectures. However, the type of questions asked was of a different nature and, in fact, those related to classroom management and organization were almost twice as many in EMI. This indicates that lecturers were concerned about students' understanding of the class organization in English, while they did not pay so much attention to this question when the classes took place in the majority of students' and both lecturers' L1. This variation in the types of questions depending on the language of instruction needs further research.

Morell (2020) highlights the paramount role that not only questioning practices but also interactional and multimodal teaching resources should play, as EMI lecturers themselves rate lectures that include more questions and both verbal and nonverbal modes of communication more positively. In any case, as Macaro (2018: 228) points out, "There is a lack of classroom interaction data at the EMI tertiary level compared to the abundance that there is on interaction in secondary classrooms." Macaro also concludes that research should not be limited to the description of how such interaction takes place, but that it should aim to examine whether higher levels of student participation entail better content and English learning.

Research on EMI has also revealed that the focus is clearly placed on content and, consequently, there is a remarkable imbalance between language and content objectives. When EMI classrooms have been looked into, all the observed lecturers pay some attention to the teaching of linguistic forms, but these forms are usually analyzed in very limited ways, which is why there is an urgent need to raise both lecturers' and students' awareness of language forms and their relevance for language teaching and learning (Costa 2012). Although the EMI lecturer should become a discourse guide of the subject taught in English, the fact is that students are usually left to work out the rules of the subject discourse for themselves (Airey 2012). Arnó-Macià and Mancho-Barés (2015) observed three different degree course classes (agronomy engineering, law, and business) and confirmed that lecturers focused their discourse almost exclusively on content, whereas episodes on language were very sporadic and connected to comprehension breakdowns.

The study by Martinez, Machado, and Palma (2021) in Brazil is worth noting in this regard. Their findings indicated that EMI lecturers felt apologetic when they were dealing with language issues (language-related episodes or LREs in the authors' terminology), but that students appreciated and found these specific instances of attention to language helpful. For example, students were particularly fond of their lecturers' use of synonymy as a type of reformulation because it helped them to grasp some specific concepts. Moreover, they interpreted it as a teaching strategy aimed at making sure they understood what was being taught and as a way to reinforce and explain vocabulary; they were especially appreciative of the lecturers' highlighting of lexis that could be confusing because of false cognates in the students' L1 (Portuguese). However, students do not consider that LREs should become very prominent in EMI classes, and ought to be reserved for particular classroom situations, as the aforementioned problems derived from cognates or key grammatical or vocabulary-related issues. Since both lecturers and students are not willing to tackle language issues in content classes, team teaching may work as a way to help students develop their English skills.

5.1.1 Team Teaching

As mentioned in Section 4.1, language learning objectives are not contemplated either in EMI lecturers' teaching or assessment practices. However, the language used in EMI classes plays a key role in the transmission of knowledge, which is why the widespread belief that language teaching falls outside the remit of EMI lecturers is paradoxical. One of the possible solutions to this dilemma lies in language and content lecturers working together, as proposed by different authors who have called for the implementation of such collaboration (Lasagabaster, 2018; Núñez Asomoza, 2015; Schmidt-Unterberger, 2018).

This approach will also help to do away with the pedagogical solitude characteristic at tertiary level, where lecturers usually work on their own in their classes, in contrast with primary and secondary education, in which the coordination between teachers is fostered to a much greater degree. This dialogue between partners has proven to turn teachers into more reflective practitioners while becoming a key component of their professional and academic development (Farrell, 2020; Shagrir, 2017). The collaboration is bidirectional. In one direction, it will help language teachers, usually experts in English for specific purposes (ESP) or English for academic puposes (EAP), to work as facilitators and advisors on language issues to content teachers. In the other direction, their language courses could be informed and updated by real EMI classes, which would help to make ESP and EAP provision more relevant through the sharing of experiences and reflections with their content teacher counterparts. This cooperation is vital if students' (and even lecturers') linguistic needs are to be identified in order to subsequently develop a plan to cater for such needs, because "EMI indeed has the potential of acting as a disciplinary language-learning driver but not as a substitute for academic and specialized language teaching" (Mancho-Barés and Aguilar-Pérez, 2020: 278).

Implementing team teaching, however, is not always straightforward and two main deterring factors could be mentioned. Firstly, the human and economic resources needed may not be at universities' disposal; some teaching staff are overwhelmed with work and are not able to participate in this endeavor because their university lacks the necessary funding to contract supporting lecturers. If funding were available, in the initial stages of EMI implementation, releases (releasing teachers from teaching to undertake specific activities such as collaborate with content teachers) should be granted so that language and content lecturers could work together on course planning. Secondly, lack of tradition is an additional stumbling block, because university practitioners are used to working in watertight compartments where there is little communication with other colleagues, let alone from a different specialization, as the roots of discipline boundaries are still deep-seated in higher education.

When lecturers and students have been surveyed about the possibility of putting team teaching into action, they usually show positive attitudes. In the opinion of undergraduates, three areas will especially benefit from this collaboration: pronunciation, oral presentations, and written production. Both lecturers and students coincide in the need for language support, as mere exposure to academic English will not be sufficient. They also consider that language support maximizes exposure to English, while exerting a positive impact on content learning and even becoming a motivational boost for some of them. Conversely, some concerns are also raised, as some stakeholders fear that the attention paid to language will be at the expense of content learning (Lasagabaster, 2021a). However, these fears can be allayed if the procedure and the goals of this collaboration are clearly established, as both lecturers and students highlight that the benefits of team teaching outweigh any potential misgivings.

Lecturers and students strongly believe that the content lecturer should control the collaboration process, and that the language lecturer should concentrate on language matters and the content lecturer on teaching content. The divide therefore is difficult to overcome, as these beliefs are strongly entrenched among EMI participants (Lasagabaster, 2021a). However, we are still missing research on the impact of this collaboration on both lecturers' and students' perspectives, and how their different backgrounds in diverse higher education institutions affect their perceptions about the usefulness of this team teaching approach. Yet, this collaboration would allow language instructors to offer lower-proficiency students additional support in EMI education, as the integration of language teaching alongside content learning would enormously help those students with less command of the language (Jiang, Zhang, & May, 2019; Rose, 2021).

Last but not least, not only does team teaching have the potential to cope with the integration of content and language objectives, but it will also help to boost the quality of EMI programs. High-quality bilingual programs should attend to the professional development of their teaching staff, an issue that leads us to the next section.

5.1.2 EMI Professional Development

Teacher professional development encompasses a wide variety of activities (e.g. a three-hour seminar, a three-day conference, a three-week workshop, or a three-year degree) in which teachers take part with a view to improving their teaching skills, knowledge, and effectiveness. However, EMI-related professional development has not been a priority of universities nor has it received much attention from EMI researchers. In fact, lecturers who are very proficient in English sometimes decide not to jump on the EMI bandwagon on the grounds that their institution provides little or no support at all.

In-service EMI lecturers demand courses or workshops that help them surf EMI implementation with greater guarantees. Different authors have proposed different approaches regarding teacher development. The framework by Rubio-Alcalá and Mallorquín (2020) accentuates the need to prepare lecturers with regard to three types of competencies: language, pedagogical, and emotional competencies. After a study carried out in China, Macaro and Han (2019) propose that professional development programs should consider three main dimensions regarding competencies: the national context and their level of international transferability, the generic competencies, and the subject-specific competencies. Other authors such as Fortanet-Gómez (2013) argue that EMI lecturers need to reflect on and consider four components: the language component (attention needs to be paid to the language utilized to transmit knowledge and classroom contents); the pedagogical component (use of adequate pedagogical tools); the cultural component (an increasing number of international students are joining EMI courses); and the human factor (the acceptance not only of one's potential linguistic limitations but also those of their students).

However, the number of studies focused on the actual impact of EMI professional development is rather scarce and their focus is primarily on language proficiency. Although rare, exceptions to this mainly language-focused norm can still be found in the literature. In Italy, Guarda and Helm (2017b) designed a professional development program and observed that lecturers benefitted from reflection on their practice. The seminar discussions and group work triggered a process of reflection in which they realized that they had to adopt a more student-centered approach. The impact was also perceived in the long run, as after nine months the lecturers were more concerned about their students' needs, the need to foster their participation, a more flexible attitude toward L1 use, and a greater use of multimodality (i.e. technology) to underpin students' understanding.

In another of the few exceptions, Tuomainen (2018) describes a scheme at a university in Finland, which was made up of pre-course needs analysis, six joints meetings, individual teaching demonstrations, and postcourse analysis. Although at the beginning of the initiative the participants were concerned about language matters, at the end of the course they found their discussions about EMI, the received corrective feedback, and their language practices in authentic situations profitable. Tuomainen points out that collective reflection helps them to be less concerned about their language proficiency while feeling more at ease. Nine lecturers participated and the results coincide with those obtained by Guarda and Helm (2017b), which seems to indicate that reflective practice is a powerful tool that contributes to the empowerment of EMI lecturers. Pagèze and Lasagabaster (2017) also verified that EMI training changed lecturers' teaching practices by making their lectures more student-centered, while it also helped them to think of English as a lingua franca and to dispel some of their concomitant fears as non-native speakers: "This is helpful because it shifts lecturer identity from being a model of linguistic perfection to a facilitator and manager of a classroom situation and places the student at the centre of learning" (308).

One of the most recent contributions to the field was provided by Borsetto and Bier (2021). They report on a professional development program called Academic Lecturing, which is run at a university in the north of Italy and consists of face-to-face seminars and online activities, alongside an individual support service. One of the most conspicuous features of the program is that it incorporates ICT training. The feedback questionnaire filled out by the forty-two participants revealed that the program had met their expectations because of two main reasons: it provided useful suggestions about teaching tools unknown to them and, once again, an opportunity to reflect on their own teaching. Regular reflection is clearly a key concept in professional development.

Farrell (2020) defines reflective practice as the practice through which EMI lecturers subject their teaching behavior to a critical analysis so that they can adapt it to their specific context. This allows them to unearth different dimensions of their teaching philosophy, principles, and theories and examine to what extent they match with their classroom practices. He proposes a framework that consists of five stages or levels of reflection:

(i) *Philosophy* explores the lecturers themselves as persons who are at the center of the art of teaching.

(ii) *Principles* digs into the lecturers' beliefs about EMI teaching and learning, which they do not always find easy to verbalize.

(iii) *Theory* focuses on the different choices a lecturer makes to put their theories into practice, that is, what particular skills they think should be taught.

(iv) *Practice* leads EMI lecturers to reflect on their actual teaching practices and to what extent they are influenced by the previous three stages. This reflection can be carried out either during the lesson, which demands here-and-now adjustments, or after it.

(v) *Beyond practice* is the final stage, in which practitioners take a critical stance through the consideration of moral, social, and political issues related to their work but which go beyond the classroom setting.

It is interesting to note the findings of a study undertaken in Spain by Roothooft (2022) involving fifty-nine EMI participants from five universities. Most paid heed only to content and disregarded language, but those that had participated in ICLHE training focused on both language and content. Discipline-related differences were also reported, as a greater proportion of humanities lecturers than STEM lecturers acknowledged having changed their teaching style as a result of participating in EMI programs. The reasons behind such differences are well worth delving into in future research.

Research on EMI should therefore consider the impact of professional development programs on EMI teaching. Lecturers are clamouring for this type of support, while institutions seek successful strategies based on empirical evidence that can be shared with their teaching staff and implemented in their own faculties. As Dafouz (2018: 550) contends, professional development programs should be "fully integrated in the institutional structure," but this is still far from reality. Governing bodies should be made aware of this so that the necessary means are eventually devoted to the much needed and demanded professional development programs.

5.2 Actual Use of English in EMI Classes

Although institutional language policies establish that English should be the means of instruction on EMI courses, generally speaking they "offer only the faintest of outlines of what is actually happening in classrooms" (van der Walt, 2013: 11). Stating that a course is EMI does not necessarily mean that English is spoken all the time and, consequently, language choice becomes a local construction (Söderlundh, 2013). There is wide evidence that lecturers and students code switch and translanguage both inside and outside the classroom, but the actual measurement of instruction carried out in English is more often than not overlooked.

In fact, one of the main limitations of studies on EMI has to do with the little information provided about how much teaching is carried out in English. In their analysis of thirty-six studies carried out in mainland China, Peng and Xie (2021) found out that only six included any information about this question, the percentage of English teaching being 50 percent or above. The remaining studies did not report any actual or estimated percentage of instruction in English. In Asia, different studies show that the use of English, despite being stipulated as the working language, is rather limited and "far from a full-fledged practice" (Jiang, Zhang, & May, 2019: 116) at some universities, whereas in Europe, English tends to be used more in all course-related activities (Wilkinson & Gabriëls, 2021). Although generalizations are always risky and unfair to some institutions, this trend seems to be confirmed by EMI literature.

Since the percentage of time that English is actually used as a means of instruction is a significant moderator of English achievement (Peng and Xie, 2021), future research should report this information in the description of the study. But if English is not used all the time, when and why is the L1 resorted to?

5.2.1 First Language Use and Translanguaging Practices in EMI

Although nominally English is expected to be the only language used as means of instruction in EMI, reality clearly shows that monolingual practices are very rare. In fact, there is a growing trend to lambast English-only language policies in EMI classes. Some voices are extremely critical of this monolingual approach and the ensuing privileged position given to English. Antia affirms that exclusive EMI, "especially one that also takes its norms for the 'E' exogenously, is an *aberration* in those countries that lie outside of the 'inner circle'" (Paulsrud, Tian, & Toth, 2021: xv; our emphasis). According to Antia, such aberration needs to be corrected in outer/expanding university contexts in Kachru's (1992) World Englishes model, as English-only strict practices run the risk of eroding EMI students' learning potential. Albeit just recently, the use of the L1 and translanguaging practices have attracted EMI researchers' attention, and there is an increasing number of studies that have analyzed this issue.

As a result of the fact that many universities do not have a language policy adapted to the EMI context, the amount of L1 use observed is very varied not only across different institutions but even within the same university (Rose, 2021; Sahan, 2019). Hardly ever do official documents make any reference to students' and lecturers' use of the L1 (Mazak & Carroll, 2017), which is why researchers have shown great interest in examining the coexistence of the L1 and English in EMI classes. Translanguaging practices are gaining momentum, and researchers have delved into the impact of flexible approaches aimed to avert the limitations of language separation or compartmentalization. Translanguaging could be defined as the use of all the speaker's linguistic and semiotic repertoire to maximize communication, that is, the use of the students' L1 resources to mediate the understanding of new concepts in English (Lin, 2016). For example, linguistic translanguaging implies that in a given university the use of the L1 alongside English would not be hampered or forbidden, although a pedagogical approach to the different languages in contact should be considered, and clear guidelines about when to use each of the languages should be established (see Muguruza, Cenoz, & Gorter, 2020). Researchers' increasing interest has led to a growing body of research on translanguaging at university level in the last few years, while most previous research in the field scrutinised the pre-university level.

At the University of the Basque Country in Spain, Doiz and Lasagabaster (2017) found that EMI lecturers were not fond of allowing use of the L1 and preferred to stick to an English-only language policy in their classes. However, they found an interesting divide between the inside and outside class behavior, as in the former translanguaging practices were avoided but in the latter they were not unusual (e.g. students' queries during tutorials). The authors conclude that EMI lecturers in this particular context were closer to a monolingual view of language codes, despite the fact that all the teachers were multilingual speakers of at least three languages. These results were attributed to two main reasons: the influence of Canadian immersion programs (in which language compartmentalization has been a characteristic feature) on the Basque education system, and the entrenched belief that the more exposure to English the higher the language competence to be achieved by students. However, in the same institution, Muguruza, Cenoz, and Gorter (2020) observed a lecturer who implemented a flexible language policy, allowing students to use the three languages in contact (Basque, Spanish, and English) to take part in class and to complete their assignments. In other words, the lecturers' input was in English, but the students' output could be in any of the three languages. The students' journals and focus group discussions indicated that students responded positively to the lecturers' linguistic flexibility, but the authors acknowledged that this approach did not promote the use of English for production. On the positive side, students were able to follow this EMI course thanks to the lecturers' pedagogical translanguaging despite their limited English proficiency. Similarly, Llanes and Cots (2020) compared English gains in a business EMI course in which a group of students followed a translanguaging approach and another group with a strictly monolingual approach. Both groups experienced language gains, but the few significant differences always favored the former, suggesting "that a plurilingual approach might be more effective than a monolingual one" (13).

Although the previous studies (Llanes & Cots, 2020; Muguruza, Cenoz, & Gorter, 2020) are based on a single EMI course and specific pedagogical translanguaging strategies, which is why results should be considered with caution, other authors have also detected the positive impact of avoiding language isolation (Mazak & Carroll, 2017). Moreover, studies undertaken in diverse contexts such as China and Japan (Rose & Galloway, 2019), Spain (Doiz & Lasagabaster, 2021), South Africa, Malawi, Cambodia, and Kazakhstan (Paulsrud, Tian, & Toth, 2021) have found that English-only teaching practices are very exceptional. In African countries that were under British rule in the twentieth century, language-in-education policies usually follow an English-only approach that places English as the sole medium of instruction. The role of English as a lingua franca and its prestige in the academic sphere has determined its hegemonic position as the only suitable language for the transmission of knowledge. Nevertheless, L1 use is widespread because it increases students' engagement with the content of the courses while facilitating interpersonal relations between teaching staff and students (Reilly, 2021).

Multilingual approaches are also the norm in educational systems that have traditionally been monolingual, such as the Japanese and Chinese university contexts, even though translanguaging practices only involve the main local language and English. In fact, it is interesting to note that the majority of Japanese (65 percent) and Chinese (70 percent) students believe that they should be allowed to use English and their mother tongue (Rose & Galloway, 2019), as do students and lecturers in the Arabian/Persian Gulf (Belhiah & Elhami, 2015; Graham, Eslami, & Hillman, 2021). In EMI Engineering classes in Turkey, Sahan, Rose, and Macaro (2021) identified four variations of EMI implementation: English-dominant and lecturer-centered, English-dominant and interactive, L1-dominant and interactive lectures, and L1-dominant and lecturer-centered. Once again, classroom observation showed that the incorporation of the L1 into EMI classes was commonplace, although differences were detected even between classes within the same department, and the L1 was used in lower proportions in elite universities. At any rate, classes were made up mostly of local students who shared the same L1, as was the case in the majority of the studies just mentioned.

Nevertheless, the use of students' L1 may be fraught with tensions if classes also encompass international students. In fact, Kuteeva (2020) observed in Sweden that translanguaging practices were not always perceived as an empowering strategy and they may even function as a mechanism of exclusion. In her study, international students felt that translingual practices yielded a feeling of inequality whenever local students' L1 was used in class, as international students did not share the same L1 linguistic resources and therefore could not take advantage of them. Similar results are reported by Kim (2017) in South Korea, where international students complain about the excessive use of Korean on the part of some instructors. In fact, Kim refers to a study in which 36.6 percent of the 1,728 professors surveyed indicated that they used Korean in 50 percent or more of their teaching, a classroom practice that, according to Kim, "can hardly be called EMI" (59).

In sum, it can be concluded that EMI researchers argue that English-only ideologies should come to a halt and language policymakers should give up establishing a monolingual perspective that does not fit with today's multilingual and multicultural university and the benefits of pedagogical translanguaging detected in the literature. In those contexts in which decision makers still remain anchored to monolingual beliefs, EMI practitioners have called for resistance and the disruption of language hierarchies, as well as for the implementation of teaching practices that help their students access knowledge rather than hinder such access. Translanguaging advocates should strive to overcome the stigmatization of mixing languages in university contexts (Mazak & Carroll, 2017), because research shows that L1 use is not a sign of a linguistic deficit, but rather a means to achieve an educational objective. As a matter of fact, some authors state that in those university contexts in which lecturers' and students'

English proficiency raises concerns, translanguaging practices could become "an alternative to ensure that the transmission of subject content is not compromised" (Peng & Xie, 2021: 14). Thus, EMI practitioners need to get to grips with the idea that having more than one language "is an advantage when engaging critically and successfully (in academic terms) with complex academic material" (van der Walt, 2013: 122).

Future research should analyze whether translanguaging can help to underpin and improve content learning in EMI classes, because this would be the best way to do away with stigmas related to language mixing. Similarly, researchers should focus on whether students and lecturers favor translanguaging in all classroom situations or whether some activities (e.g. class discussions and small group work) are more positively viewed than others (e.g. assignments and exams; see Section 7). Similarly, since Graham, Eslami, and Hillman (2021) found that Arabic L1 students indicated positive attitudes toward translanguaging in political science and history but less favorable attitudes in maths, it would be interesting to study whether some specializations are more prone to accept translingual practices than others.

6 Impact of EMI on Learning

This section will look at two main aspects of EMI research, language learning and content learning, as EMI is believed to contribute to students' English language proficiency with no cost to content learning. However, it is worth remembering that, while the teaching of language and content in an integrated manner is one of the main tenets of the CLIL approach at pre-university levels, this principle is alien to EMI, and explicit references to such integration are rarely found in EMI at university. If explicit language objectives are excluded from EMI courses, does EMI actually have any positive impact on students' English proficiency?

6.1 Language Learning

Although some authors (Chapple, 2015) warn against the naïve equation of EMI with an automatic improvement in English proficiency, many university authorities, policymakers, and decision makers accept it on faith. Ironically, governing bodies tend to presuppose that either all participants are proficient in English to the extent that they can grasp complex university content delivered in a foreign language, or if this were not the case, EMI courses will help to make up for any linguistic deficiencies they may suffer from. This is based on the widely held belief that language learning will take place implicitly simply by students being exposed to English on EMI courses (Weimberg & Symon, 2017), which is why

"English is not taught but is nonetheless expected to be learned" (Pecorari & Malmström, 2018a: 511).

The number of studies aimed at measuring the development of English in EMI courses is rather limited. In addition, many of them were based on lecturers' and students' holistic impressions, while others relied on small samples and were exploratory in nature. From those that actually measured English proficiency, counted on a reasonably large sample, and performed statistical analyses to test significant improvement, two main groups can be distinguished, depending on whether they focused on specific language skills (Aguilar & Muñoz, 2014; Chostelidou & Griva, 2014; Chou, 2018; Richter, 2019) or on general English proficiency (Hernández-Nanclares & Jiménez-Muñoz, 2017; Lei & Hu, 2014; Rogier, 2012; Yang, 2015).

It is striking how diverse the results obtained turned out to be. In the case of the first group, in Aguilar and Muñoz's study (2014) EMI students completed pre- and posttests and scored higher in listening and grammar after being enrolled on seven different courses. However, this improvement was detected only in the case of students with the lowest level of proficiency, while the higher proficiency students did not benefit from EMI. The authors underscore that out of the seven lecturers participating in the study, two had a lower intermediate command of English, three upper intermediate, one advanced, and one very advanced. According to the authors, in these conditions some lecturers could not provide rich input and only students below the intermediate level took advantage of the experience. Chostelidou and Griva (2014) compared EMI and non-EMI students in reading comprehension and the results showed statistically significant differences in favor of EMI students. Chou (2018) compared full EMI and partial EMI programs and their impact on students' speaking development. Full EMI students were significantly better because they had more exposure and more opportunities to communicate in English. All the three studies that analyzed the development of specific language skills were carried out after a semester, but they all compared different language skills (grammar and listening; reading; speaking) and the comparisons were carried out between different types of groups (the same students longitudinally; EMI vs. non-EMI; full EMI vs. partial EMI).

Richter's (2019) study makes an original contribution because it spans six semesters and focuses on the development of pronunciation among EMI students, one of their main concerns, as seen in Section 4.2. The Austrian undergraduates were enrolled in an EMI program in which up to 50 percent of the courses were delivered in English by mainly native speakers. Even though instruction was clearly focused on content, EMI students' pronunciation improved significantly more than that of the control group. Although the study shows some limitations (e.g. EMI participants were more proficient and more motivated) and the setting may not be comparable to that of many universities that do not count on so many native speakers, the findings indicate that this approach can contribute to improving pronunciation.

In the case of studies that examined students' general English proficiency, the second group, the results were as diverse as in the case of the first group. In Rogier's (2012) study significant gains were found in the four language skills after a four-year EMI program, but especially so in speaking. Although students were expected to graduate with a 6.0 IELTS score, on average they only improved half a band and achieved a score of 5.5. These poor results led the university to put into action a pilot program with support from language lecturers. Lei and Hu (2014) compared EMI and non-EMI students after a year and no differences in their English proficiency were found. The authors attribute these daunting results to different reasons, such as an inefficient implementation of EMI, instructors' Inadequate English proficiency, and poor pedagogical strategies. Yang (2015) measured EMI students' language development through pre- and post-general English tests after two years and compared their results with those of non-EMI students using national-level measurements. The former outperformed the latter in receptive skills but not in productive ones, which the authors put down to the fact that EMI courses were lecture-based and students had no possibility of practicing their productive skills. Lastly, in the only study that was not conducted in the Asian context in this second group, Hernández-Nanclares and Jiménez-Muñoz (2017) undertook a study in a low-intensity EMI group (one EMI subject per semester) during two semesters in Spain. Students self-assessed their command of English in the four language skills, which were then objectively assessed. The objective measures showed a significant improvement in all language skills, but especially in reading. However, the objective measurement was not as positive as students' self-assessment. It has to be noted that the content lecturer collaborated with a native language expert and a linguist and teacher trainer, which would help to explain the positive results despite it being a low-intensity EMI program.

In sum, the studies in this second group (general English proficiency) found a positive language development in receptive skills above all (Hernández-Nanclares and Jiménez-Muñoz, 2017; Lei & Hu, 2014; Yang, 2015), except in Rogier's (2012) study, in which the students improved mainly their speaking skills. However, this was also the longest study (lasting four years, while the others were over one or two years).

Despite the heterogeneity of all the studies included in the first and second groups, three factors stand out. First, the intensity of the EMI program has to be taken into account, as those studies that found a more positive impact were those that included higher-intensity programs. A single EMI subject per semester does not seem to be very effective for language learning. Second, the pedagogical practices implemented play a key role. Whereas inefficient teaching strategies unsurprisingly lead to negative outcomes (Lei and Hu, 2014), some rewarding teaching experiences can be articulated, such as the collaboration between content and language lecturers (Hernández-Nanclares and Jiménez-Muñoz, 2017), the results of which indicate that methodological adjustments are needed to benefit language learning. And third, there is a need to reconsider the instruments designed to measure language proficiency. The tests used in these studies are not tailored to EMI courses and are usually very focused on language knowledge while neglecting more communicative abilities and disciplinary knowledge. Most of the tasks included in language tests such as IELTS are not adequate and do not elicit the academic language characteristic of EMI courses (Tedick & Cammarata, 2012). In fact, Airey (2015) affirms that the discipline in which the data was collected may prove more important than the country where EMI studies are undertaken, which is why disciplinary literacies should be borne in mind (Kuteeva & Airey, 2014). That is, the language required to learn engineering may be very different to the language needed in history. One of the main alleged benefits of EMI lies in the fact that it fosters disciplinary language and prepares students to deal with the specialized English they will need for their future professional careers, but hardly ever is this measured in traditional general English proficiency tests.

Particularly worthy of attention is a study by Peng and Xien (2021). In a meta-analysis of EMI studies constrained to mainland China from 2000 to 2020, these researchers compared English language achievement in EMI and Chinese-medium instruction (CMI) groups. Their review included thirty-six studies involving forty-four independent samples. English achievement was measured in twelve of those independent samples and EMI students outstripped their CMI counterparts with a large effect size. Since almost 75 percent of the samples were from medical disciplines and this could bias the results, they decided to exclude these disciplines from another round of analyses, for these students are required to invest more effort in their very demanding disciplines in which English plays an important role, considering the globalization of medical studies. Nonetheless, in the case of disciplines other than medical disciplines, EMI students still achieved higher English scores (with a significant and medium effect size). But not only were the differences between EMI and CMI significantly moderated according to discipline, but also by research design (the randomized controlled trial produced the largest differences) and English instruction time (when it was above 50 percent better results were yielded).

In fact, translanguaging is also worth considering in this regard, as it is aimed at enhancing students' learning (see Section 5.2.1).

The conclusion to be drawn is that the purported foreign language learning advantages that, according to some voices, are inherent to EMI programs have only been partially detected in the studies carried out so far. This is why further research needs to consider the three factors mentioned earlier (intensity of EMI programs, teacher collaboration, and reconsideration of the tools to measure language proficiency) to have a neater picture of the actual impact of EMI.

6.2 Content Learning

Not only are there even fewer studies on content learning than those focused on language learning, but they are even more limited. As in Section 6.1, this section will only consider those studies that have actually measured the impact of EMI on content learning (lecturers' and students' beliefs and self-assessment have been dealt with in Sections 4.1 and 4.2) and that have samples that are reasonably large.

Joe and Lee (2013) examined lecture comprehension by means of pre- and posttests during EMI and Korean-medium medical lectures. The three lectures under scrutiny were delivered by the same Korean lecturer, who taught half of each lecture first in English and the other half in Korean. The results indicated that the teaching language did not have any effect on the students' lecture comprehension, nor had it any impact the students' general English proficiency. However, Macaro et al. (2018) warn that the content difficulty levels of each half of the lecture were not matched, which would have allowed the author to ensure that the means of instruction was the only independent variable. Similarly, the students' level of English at the pre-stage of the study was not controlled either.

In Austria, a study by Tatzl and Messnarz (2013) looked at two groups of aeronautical engineering degree undergraduates and their written solutions to physics and mathematical problems in an exam. One group had the exam in German, the other in English. The groups were not leveled at the pretest stage, although the authors consider that since they were randomly chosen, no differences could be expected. The authors hypothesized that English would constitute a barrier to comprehension and would entail pedagogical consequences (additional time needed, a reduction in content and number of problems solved, or more language training or auxiliary means such as dictionaries). However, when the results were compared, no differences were observed, irrespective of whether the student answered the problem posed in German or in English. Tatzl and Messnarz argue that a B2 level is enough to solve problems in English, although they also acknowledge that "it remains difficult to measure whether failure to solve a physics problem is due to deficiencies in English as the foreign language or deficiencies in physics and mathematics" (628). Since no text answers were required (the solutions were numerical), productive skills in the form of text answers still need to be researched, as more language-dependent examinations may lead to different results.

Dafouz, Camacho, and Urquia (2014) compared two groups of Spanish students who were enrolled on an EMI Business Administration degree. The EMI group and the Spanish-medium group were matched on university entrance exam scores and their results in three subjects contrasted at the end of the term. The results did not find any significant difference and the authors concluded that EMI did not have any negative impact on content learning. However, they also acknowledged that the results need to be treated with caution because of the limited size of data, the reduced access to classroom practices, and its focus on a single higher education institution.

In the aforementioned meta-analysis by Peng and Xien (2021), EMI students significantly outperformed their CMI counterparts, which was "unexpected and somewhat inconsistent with the general view on the effectiveness of EMI found in the literature" (10). When once again medical disciplines were excluded from the analysis to avoid any possible bias, no significant differences were detected, which would concur with the studies previously reviewed in this section, since the initial significant effect of EMI on content learning was due to the students enrolled in medical disciplines.

Therefore, once medical students are excluded, all the studies undertaken in nonmedical disciplines are homogeneous in terms of academic achievement and lead us to conclude that there is no evidence to indicate that EMI harms students' academic performance when compared to their L1-medium counterparts in contexts as diverse as Austria, Spain, China, or South Korea. The characteristics of universities delivering EMI are so manifold that it is difficult to arrive at general conclusions based on the results obtained in a particular institution. Nevertheless, and broadly speaking, the results available so far allow us to conclude that EMI should not hamper content learning if programs are cogently designed and implemented. The available evidence points in this direction and can be deemed reassuring for all EMI stakeholders, including lecturers, students, and decision makers, but further studies are needed.

Since several of the studies on the impact of EMI on language and content knowledge development miss some basic information, such as the percentage of instruction in English, or provide a poor description of both the sample and the research instruments, future research should try to overcome these methodological issues.

6.3 The Interaction between (Academic) Language Proficiency and Content Learning

Some studies have explored the impact of English proficiency on content learning and, therefore, on students' success in EMI programs. In Japanese higher education, Rose and colleagues (2020) found that English proficiency was the strongest predictor of success in EMI international business, and that less proficient students were at a disadvantage. These findings led the authors to claim that these disadvantaged students should not see their chances to participate in EMI limited, since they were willing to take the plunge, but language support should be provided to make up for their linguistic limitations. Students' English proficiency was measured both through ESP grades and general proficiency (the Test of English for International Communication), but the former produced stronger correlations with success (which was operationalized in terms of content exam scores). This is why, according to these researchers, language support should focus on specialized vocabulary and academic/content-related needs.

In the Chinese university context, Xie and Curle (2019) also explored the impact of Business English proficiency, motivation, and perceived success on academic success in EMI. Once again, content-related English proficiency (Business English proficiency rather than general English competence) emerged as the strongest predictor, and, as was also the case in Rose and colleagues' (2020) study, motivation did not correlate with success in EMI. In an EMI economics program at a public Turkish university, Curle and colleagues (2020) measured English proficiency using an adapted version of the Cambridge Preliminary English Test (PET), a B1 level of practical language skills for everyday use. General English proficiency turned out not to be a significant predictor and, in fact, it accounted for only 0.3 percent of the variance in EMI course scores.

What is interesting about these three studies (Curle et al., 2020; Rose et al., 2020 and Xie & Curle, 2019) is that general English proficiency does not exert a significant influence on EMI success and that higher education institutions should pay attention to academic English. The qualitative data apportioned by Curle and colleagues (2020) also underpins this, as students demanded academic language support, in particular in relation to technical or academic vocabulary, results that concur with those obtained by Lasagabaster, Doiz, and Pavón (2018) among Spanish EMI students, who also raised the need to enhance their academic vocabulary. Evans and Morrison's (2011a) large-scale study would also tally with the previous ones. In their mixed-methods study, these authors interviewed twenty-eight students over their three years of study and surveyed around 3,000 students enrolled in EMI in Hong Kong. Their findings indicated that students experienced four main problems (technical vocabulary, lecture comprehension, achievement of an appropriate academic style, and meeting disciplinary needs), all of them aspects related to discipline-specific academic language.

The vital role of academic language in EMI courses has been underscored by many authors (e.g. Basturkmen, 2019; Mälmstrom, Pecorari, & Gustafsson, 2016) and all these results only support the need to provide students with the English necessary for disciplinary study. How subject-specific language and literacies favor content learning was also confirmed by Sánchez-Pérez (2021) in a study in Spain in which she observed a positive relationship between the occurrence of disciplinary-literacy variables (e.g. cohesive devices, use of the passive voice, and technical words) and EMI students' content proficiency in writing. In light of this high degree of agreement, the following conclusion by Curle and colleagues (2020: 9) is well worth considering:

> Many, if not all, universities in Turkey, similar to some other EMI settings around the globe, provide general English courses in their Intensive English programmes to prepare students to study through EMI. Our findings demonstrate that general English language proficiency may not be as beneficial as academic proficiency to overall success in EMI. Students should therefore rather be exposed to more Academic English courses in such preparatory programmes.

In addition, students will learn the specific language of their discipline, which will be very profitable in their future academic and professional careers. As for future research, longitudinal studies would be welcomed to track EMI students' English development supported by specially designed academic language courses.

7 Assessment in EMI

Researchers on EMI have not paid much attention to assessment so far, as reflected in the limited number of studies on this topic. This is despite the fact that assessment is one of the issues that EMI lecturers are more concerned about, as the following quotation from Ball and Lindsay (2013: 56) reflects:

> I feel that students taking courses in a foreign language should be treated differently when assessing how well they are doing. I put most of my effort into providing them with formative assessment ... Overall I am worried about the fairness of the assessment criteria. The contents are exactly the same, as are the learning objectives, but in terms of competences and skills, I believe that different criteria of assessment should be applied.

When assessment is considered in the literature, two main questions stand out: Should both language and content be evaluated? Should translanguaging practices be allowed in assignments and exams?

In the case of the first question, EMI scholars tend to show a flexible perspective when considering the evaluation of language in EMI programs (the evaluation of content is taken for granted because it is vital in content subjects). The general view could be summarized in Fortanet-Gómez's (2013) proposal with regard to written and oral tests. She proposes that students should be provided with feedback in order to help them improve their English language use, but in the case of written tests content lecturers should:

> only focus on communication as an aim and the use of specific terminology and discourse, disregarding the precise correction of language mistakes. In oral tests, aspects that have been regarded as characteristic of multilinguals, such as occasional code-switching, or some non-standard uses of the language which do not hinder communication, should not be penalised. (233)

It is worth noting that both lecturers and students agree that language aspects should not be considered in their final marks. Lecturers on EMI programs usually put forward three arguments to explain their refusal to penalize language mistakes when marking students' work (Doiz et al., 2019): (i) they do not perceive themselves as English teachers and consider that language issues fall outside their remit; (ii) they are mainly concerned with the subject matter; and (iii) they do not view themselves as capable of marking the students' English. This is a clear indication that EMI stakeholders regard English as the vehicle for content teaching but not as an end in itself. Their main concern usually lies in the fact that they do not see themselves as capable of evaluating students' oral and written production as if it were in their L1, in which language adequacy may influence their assessment of content learning, especially when language issues hinder comprehension.

In their handbook for EMI at university in Israel, Lawrence, Inbar-Lourie, and Weinberg (2017: 28–29) state that EMI policy implementation "must relate in part to assessment issues" and that "[d]ecisions on the course assignments can be undertaken in consultation with the language department so that demands on the students are reasonable in light of their linguistic capabilities." Following the example of Maastricht university, these authors contend that the areas to be assessed should be the joint responsibility of each faculty and the university's language centre. Once experience is gained by the faculties, the role of the language centre should become more advisory. However, as Ball and Lindsay (2013: 59) put it, the content teacher should not be asked in any case "to change identity but to merely consider the impact that language and discourse might have on his/her area." In order to achieve this, Lawrence, Inbar-Lourie, and Weinberg propose the use of standardized marking rubrics that should be given to students so that they get to know what they need to produce and how they are going to be assessed. Interestingly, Block and Mancho-Barés (2021) explored the rubrics used by two EMI lecturers to evaluate students' oral presentations and found evidence that both lecturers foregrounded the assessment of language despite asserting that this was not their responsibility as EMI instructors. However, the rubrics did not provide any washback effect on their teaching, as students were not offered sufficient practice for oral presentations and for producing English in extended discourse. These findings led the authors to conclude that professional development programs should also include assessment procedures.

As far as the second question is concerned, Dearden (2015) highlights that her informants from fifty-five different countries described assessment as problematic, as it is not always obvious in which language exams should be held. The different situations this author found ranged from university contexts, in which the lectures were delivered mainly in the L1 but assessment was in English, to contexts in which lectures were in English but exams were completed in the L1 because of different reasons: university policy, student pressure, or even legal issues (exams could only be carried out in the L1). In France, for example, the Toubon law (1994) imposed restrictions on the use of English in education and stipulated that French was the only language for teaching. These legal restrictions, although widely ignored in many universities, were adjusted by the Fioraso law in 2013 and teaching in languages other than French was officially allowed in higher education (Pagèze & Lasagabaster, 2017).

When talking about students' evaluation, translanguaging immediately springs to mind. Van der Walt (2013) proposes translanguaging as a pedagogical tool that could help to improve assessment practices in EMI courses. She acknowledges that the management of assessment of academic essays that include more than one language can become challenging, but she also poses a possible course of action: "One requirement could be that students use well-formed, academic discourse, whatever the language may be" (157). In those university contexts in which students' English proficiency is not so high, as is the case in some African university settings, the author considers that students should be given the opportunity to complete tests and assignments in their stronger language. In this way, they would build on their receptive English proficiency while having an option to fend off the insecurities derived from the feeling of not being able to express themselves successfully in English in one of the most stress-provoking university tasks. This flexible approach would help to underpin equity in learning conditions while avoiding potential linguistic hurdles associated with learning content through "a language that is not fully familiar to students" (Shohamy, 2013: 203).

According to Mazak and Carroll (2017), policymakers and university instructors should not uncritically embrace market-based reforms that focus solely on standardized assessments and globalized metrics that allow the use of only one language. Language policies should consider the possibility of translanguaging in assessment tasks without penalizing those students who fall back on their whole linguistic repertoire. Since the dictum that "content learning prevails over English language development" is widely accepted by EMI content lecturers, it is hard to understand why some lecturers remain so reluctant toward translanguaging practices. The aforementioned "Plan of Action for Multilingualism" put into action by the Pompeu Fabra University (2007) is an attempt to foster translanguaging practices in assessment tasks. According to regulations, students are allowed to use any of the three languages in contact – Catalan, Spanish, and English – in their academic performance, although assessment tasks will always be presented in English (but students can answer in the language of their choice).

Translanguaging is sometimes also permitted in some African universities. Hibbert and van der Walt (2014) report that, according to some Afrikaans institutions' language policies, students are allowed to choose Afrikaans or English in assignments and tests. However, since the majority of lecturers are predominantly white and bilingual in Afrikaans and English, the use of African languages is still rather limited. Nonetheless, these authors believe that the introduction of translanguaging practices in different universities may become "the precursor to the increased use of African languages in formal, written assessments" (215).

However, Doiz and Lasagabaster (2017) observed that Spanish instructors prefer to avoid translanguaging practices in assessment tasks. In contrast, in their analysis of assessment practices at a university in South Africa, a context in which EMI reigns supreme in all higher levels of education, Luckett and Hurst-Harosh (2021) point out that translanguaging is spreading rapidly as a result of a social desire to transform a higher education system that has been characterized as colonial, white, and elitist. The authors proved that by giving students the opportunity to translanguage in an essay that formed part of the course evaluation, students became emotionally involved, which was conducive to learning. Their chapter is part of a truly international volume that includes several underrepresented contexts the world over (Paulsrud, Tian, & Toth, 2021) and that delves into the interface between translanguaging and EMI. Despite the pervasive presence of recalcitrant monolingual ideologies, the contributors clearly attest that exclusive use of English in assessment tasks is unnatural, unrealistic and, on too many occasions, harmful, while translangua-ging, if cogently theorized and implemented (not at any cost), is legitimized as a natural, reasonable, and beneficial practice. The contributors recommend moving beyond translanguaging practices in classroom talk only to include them also in assessment tasks, especially when students share a common language. However, it has to be pointed out that some authors are not so positive and have warned about the transformative limits of translanguaging, while affirming that it may be less critical and transformational than has been sug-gested (see Jaspers, 2018).

To conclude, it can be affirmed that assessment is a key aspect that has hitherto been largely underestimated in research on EMI at university. Many questions remain to be addressed, such as whether ELF should be promoted instead of inner-circle varieties (Murata, 2019), whether translanguaging should be considered (Mazak & Carroll, 2017), what international students' stance would be were the use of the home students' L1 allowed in exams, whether EMI lecturers would be prone to accept nonstandard forms of evaluation, whether multilingual practices are viable in classes where many different L1s coexist, etc. In this vein, Hultgren and colleagues (2022) suggest that assessment should be reconceptualized "as a tool for enhancing learning by emphasizing and raising stakeholders' awareness of the important role of language" (118). According to these authors, a practical way forward would consist in granting language a more prominent role in current assessment practices, which could be boosted through language and content experts' collaboration. However, as Hultgren and colleagues (2022) acknowledge, research is direly needed to prove that assessment can enhance and improve learning in higher education, while it is also vital to secure the institutional support of policymakers and key stakeholders to put language-sensitive assessment into practice. The ever increasing diversity of EMI undoubtedly poses many challenges when it comes to assessment practices, but unfortunately there is still not much in the EMI literature about this topic.

8 Some Key Readings

In this section, I will present some key EMI readings. Due to space constraints, other interesting titles that could undoubtedly have been included have not (Block & Khan, 2021; Bradford & Brown, 2017a; Doiz, Lasagabaster, & Sierra, 2013a; Fortanet-Gómez, 2013; Richter, 2019; Sánchez-Pérez, 2020; Smit, 2010; Valcke & Wilkinson, 2017; Wilkinson & Walsh, 2015; to name but a few). This is mainly because their focus is on a single institution or country, or because other volumes by the same author(s) have already been included in this section. And for the same reason (the word limit of the Elements series), special issues on EMI in higher education (Doiz & Lasagabaster, 2020; Kuteeva, 2011; Pecorari & Malmström, 2018b; Ruiz de Zarobe & Lyster, 2018) have not been considered, but the reader is well advised to peruse them. The only exception among special issues in journals is the edited volume by Darquennes, du Plessis and Soler (2020), because, to my knowledge, this is one of the few attempts to include details of EMI programs in African universities. Since EMI literature regarding Africa is scarce, I believe its incorporation is fully justified. In fact, Macaro and colleagues (2018: 45), in their systematic review of EMI in higher education, underscore that investigations "were carried out in all geographical regions with the exception of Africa." At any rate, the selected volumes represent a recent and comprehensive view of what EMI currently looks like and what issues need to be addressed and further researched. The main issues dealt with in each of the volumes are summarized and presented in chronological order in this section.

Dearden (2015) carried out the first attempt to map the size and future trends of EMI from a global perspective. She relied on British Council staff from countries around the world as informed participants and managed to garner information about fifty-five countries. Although the results of the study should be considered with caution because they represent the view of one British Council representative for each country, some interesting trends were detected. The information gathered through open-ended questionnaires indicated that EMI provision is undergoing a rapid expansion, but it is nonetheless more widespread at tertiary level than in secondary education, with private institutions offering more courses than public ones. The main concerns were that students with a lower socioeconomic status may have more limited access to education, and that the L1 and national identity may be upstaged and undermined by English. All this leads Dearden to conclude that there is dire need for a research-driven approach by giving voice to the key stakeholders and analyzing the impact of EMI on academic and language-related outcomes.

Macaro (2018) undertook a comprehensive approach to EMI by including not only EMI at university level but also a pre-university level (secondary education). Due to the clear focus of this Element on tertiary education, I will focus on those topics that are more clearly linked to university. The book approaches EMI from a range of different angles, such as applied linguistics, second language acquisition, educational linguistics, and English language teaching, and always with a global view in mind. Not only does the volume include the perspective of lecturers and students, but it also incorporates that of policymakers. In addition, terminological issues (the thorny issue of the relationship between CLIL and EMI being a very good case in point), language policies, the type of English used in EMI, a cost–benefit analysis of its implementation, interaction in EMI classes, the connection between teacher development programs and institutional quality, learning outcomes, teacher training, and learner strategies are also covered. Throughout the book, Macaro manages to put under the spotlight the problems found in EMI research and policymaking and forces the reader to be critical about what has been written so far in this field of enquiry. Macaro ends by calling for better partnerships between researchers and policymakers on the one hand, and between content lecturers and language specialists on the other.

As editor, Murata (2019) starts from the premise that ELF is the type of English used in EMI, since this is the English used between speakers with different L1s. This edited volume is divided into three sections. The first section zooms in on the macro level, specifically on English language policies; the second is focused on the micro level and delves into lecturers' and students' voices, their identity formation, as well as classroom practices; and the third encompasses both the macro and the micro levels by presenting case studies of EMI at East Asian universities and a final chapter on ELF assessment. Although the fifteen chapters that make up the volume are focused on European, Brazilian, and Asian contexts, it could be labelled as Asia-centric, since EMI in Japan predominates with eight chapters, in addition to one chapter on EMI in China and another on EMI in South Korea. The volume succeeds in merging ELF and EMI, and helps to provide examples of its implication not only for language policy but also for pedagogy.

Unlike the other publications included in this section, which are authored by applied linguists or educational linguists, the next reference is authored by sociolinguists and provides a more sociolinguistic approach to the EMI phenomena by focusing on language diversity management from a practical perspective. Darquennes, du Plessis, and Soler (2020) edited a special issue of the journal *Sociolinguistica* in which both European, Asian, and African EMI university contexts are represented. The editors present an analytical framework aimed at both sociolinguists and university administrators, with the objective of capturing the complex and varied sociolinguistic nature of today's universities. The rest of the contributors examine language use and language policy at university level by paying special attention to the role of English and EMI with regard to different issues: the marketization of higher education, language ideologies, the implementation of legal measures, the design of language policies aimed at raising the institutional status of local languages to a status comparable to that of English, or the role of language planning agencies in higher education in South Africa.

In their co-authored volume, Dafouz and Smit (2020) introduce the term EMEMUS (English Medium Education in Multilingual University Settings) with a view to including diverse pedagogical approaches, research agendas, and different types of education (e.g. online teaching) that, in their view, other labels fail to comprise. They provide the theoretical underpinnings of the ROAD-MAPPING framework, and explain how it can help to capture the inherent diversity and complexity of international university contexts in a structured way. The framework comprises six dimensions that make up the acronym: roles of English (RO), academic disciplines (AD), (language) management (M), agents (A), practices and processes (PP), and internationalization and glocalization (ING). The book fosters discussion across disciplinary boundaries and presents practical applications of the framework to illustrate its potential based on past studies from diverse international university contexts that have used it. The authors finally suggest how ROAD-MAPPING could be used in future research.

The volume edited by Wilkinson and Gabriëls (2021) provides a broad perspective of the impact of Englishization and EMI implementation on European universities by focusing on fifteen countries and regions from Northern, Southern, Eastern and Western Europe. The different contributors address the impact of Englishization on the quality of education and research at higher education institutions as well as on the cultural identity of a region or country. They also tackle the inequality that may arise between stakeholders, the need to pay more attention to linguistic justice in the research on Englishization of universities, or the risk of stakeholders' voices being stifled by top-down language policies. Despite being a Euro-centric compendium, the authors also present the challenges that countries across the world have to face when it comes to implementing EMI programs. In fact, it is interesting to note that the debates concerning Englishization presented in this volume can also be found in many university contexts all over the world.

The last volume is a recent one edited by Lasagabaster and Doiz (2021) in which different authors from Asia, Latin America, and Europe provide an overview of classroom practices that include the resources, approaches, and materials that EMI lecturers use to deal with language-related issues in their lectures. Since one of EMI lecturers' objectives is to make their students familiar with the discourse of their respective disciplines, and gain literacy in them, while they learn the subject content, their disengagement from language is simply not possible. The different authors focus on how to foster reflection on the importance of paying heed to language aspects in EMI teaching. To do this, each chapter looks first at research findings to later help the reader translate their findings into practice, so that EMI lecturers find themselves in a stronger position to make optimal choices in their teaching. Thus, all the chapters end up with a section on recommendations for teaching practice aimed at making teachers more aware of the key role that language plays in their teaching of content, and at boosting reflective processes to help them make the necessary changes to consider language issues in their teaching.

These selected readings offer a general overview of EMI from a global perspective (Dearden, 2015), while those readers interested in zooming in on particular contexts will find more specific Asia-centric (Murata, 2019) and Euro-centric (Wilkinson & Gabriëls, 2021) accounts. Similarly, these volumes tackle EMI from different angles, including a more sociolinguistic approach (Darquennes, du Plessis & Soler, 2020), an applied linguistics perspective (Macaro, 2018), a theoretical framework to explore EMI (Dafouz & Smit, 2020), or a more microlevel perspective focused on actual classroom practices while giving practical guidance for EMI practitioners (Lasagabaster & Doiz, 2021).

9 Conclusions

There is no doubt that higher education has become the most internationalized level of education. Albeit not new, and traceable from the very inception of universities, internationalization has reached an unparalleled level and has led to an increase of multilingual practices, EMI being one of the most outstanding ones. In any case, there is widespread agreement about the fact that EMI has been mainly driven by market rather than educational forces. However, internationalization does not always equal EMI. As Belyaeva and colleagues (2021) point out, it certainly does not in Russia, as only 11.3 percent of international students enrolled in one of the most important universities studied on EMI programs. Moreover, the majority of international students come from the former republics of the Soviet Union, and want to learn and practice Russian and take courses in which Russian is the means of instruction. A similar situation can be found in many other European universities, where foreign students are attracted to learn the local language, especially if this is an international language with a high status (Lasagabaster, 2021b), as is the case with German and Italian students attending Spanish universities (and vice versa). A focus on EMI should not prevent us from seeing the forest for the trees.

Terminological confusion is a salient feature in this field of inquiry. I firmly believe that the use of EMI should be limited to higher education, whereas "CLIL in English" should be applied to primary and secondary education. In this way, readers will immediately identify what the researcher is referring to.

Because what is the point of including CLIL in the title of an article to end up concluding that the actual integration of language and content is hardly found at tertiary level? Dafouz and Smit (2021) propose the replacement of the acronym EMI by EME, substituting the I for "instruction" with an E for "education." According to these authors, the use of English as a means of instruction includes a wide range of curricular activities that constitute education (and not only instruction), and therefore EMI is deemed conceptually narrower. Only time will tell whether the acronym EME eventually replaces EMI, but for the time being EMI is clearly most widely used in the literature and that is the reason it is used throughout this Element.

Although Europe leads the way in EMI courses, Asian countries (especially China and South Korea) are introducing programs at a fast rate, whereas EMI is less habitual in Africa and South America, a great divide between elite and public universities being also noticeable. South American and African perspectives, for example, are not often heard and should be incorporated into EMI literature. As a matter of fact, most research is located in Europe and Asia, but especially in the former, because European countries were early risers in their attempt to attract international students and their higher education institutions "are in the forefront of this trend" (Murata, 2019: 1). This research imbalance needs to be addressed, and more space should be given to other contexts beyond Europe and Asia.

What emerges from this Element is the immense diversity of EMI programs. Despite such heterogeneity of experiences, many commonalities can be found between different university settings. In fact, the connecting thread lies in the impact of EMI on many different spheres of university life and how it affects the ecology of languages: more precisely, how EMI impinges on multilingual practices, policy planning issues, and the whole university community (mainly on lecturers and students, but not only them). In the last two decades, EMI has been clearly boosted by higher education institutions' desire to become competitive in the national and international spheres, but teacher training, pedagogical issues, and methodological implications still remain largely disregarded, irrespective of the continent (O'Dowd, 2018; Sahan et al., 2021).

Institutions must be aware that, if they want their EMI programs to be effective, content lecturers demand language support and institutional language policymakers should be open to providing it. Language plays a paramount role in any teaching practice, but its role is even starker when the means of instruction is a language other than students' L1, which is why *all EMI lecturers are language teachers*, whether they agree or disagree with the previous statement. As Malmström and Pecorari (2021: 213) put it:

[E]ven if *learning English* (or learning language) is not always understood by stakeholders to be an objective in EMI, and even if EMI teachers have few (if any) articulated linguistic goals for their students (cf. Airey, 2020), it *must* nonetheless be an objective in EMI (like any education, regardless of medium of instruction) that students learn to engage in *disciplinary discourse* and develop *disciplinary literacy* (emphasis in the original).

As a result of this, English language teachers should not become redundant because there are specific academic language needs that only they will be able to tackle, as content lecturers will be neither willing nor prepared to teach them. Courses in ESP and EAP should thus remain, and their vital role should be acknowledged (for the intersection between EMI and ESP, see the article by Dafouz, 2021). In addition to this, it is worth pointing out that only by taking into account content lecturers' and EMI students' viewpoints will applied linguists' recommendations have the chance to become relevant and eventually succeed in providing profitable advice. At a time when the word *interdisciplinarity* has become a mantra at university level, it is high time to actually foster it and put content lecturer and language lecturer collaboration into practice (Lasagabaster, 2018, 2021).

In their systematic review, Macaro and colleagues (2018) warn against the widespread implementation of EMI programs without reflecting on the implications. The wide body of international research reviewed in this Element demonstrates that teaching methodology (Airey, 2012; Lasagabaster & Doiz, 2021; Wilkinson, 2013) plays a vital role in the quality of EMI programs. In particular, EMI instructors should aim at implementing a student-centered approach adapted to the specific classroom context that compensates for the extra cognitive load that using English as medium of instruction places on both learners and lecturers. This is why scaffolding, group dynamics (interaction tends to be less spontaneous), and the use of multimodal resources take on even more importance. Although EMI is subject to the constraints of the local context, it can also become a driving force for change. The development of EMI teachers should thus "help lecturers appreciate EMI as a specific classroom teaching situation which is enabled by an academic and disciplinary expertise in communication, since it is this expertise which enables the teaching of the discipline through English" (Pagèze & Lasagabaster, 2017: 297).

Our review of the impact of EMI on language and content learning reveals that there are hitherto few cogently designed studies and that their results are far from being conclusive. Programs should go hand in hand with research on EMI's effect on teaching and learning processes. Authorities have shown enthusiasm over the spread of EMI and many of them have fueled high expectations around its positive outcomes. However, few institutions have left room for a careful consideration of the potential side effects it may provoke. The study by Lueg and Lueg (2015) is worth noting at this stage. The authors observed that students from higher social classes and with higher perceived English proficiency chose EMI over Danish-medium instruction, which could be interpreted as a perpetuation of social inequality, as has also been found in the Chinese context by Hu and Lei (2014), who affirm that EMI accentuates educational inequalities in China. At any rate, Lueg and Lueg (2015) conclude that their research should not be interpreted as opposing EMI, because they believe it would be to the detriment not only of students but also to the broader economy. In their opinion, students from lower social classes should be helped to overcome the barriers that EMI may erect, for example, by stressing in course descriptions that the comprehensibility of students' English is what really matters.

If all students are to benefit from EMI so that it does not become a gatekeeper that keeps out certain students, this type of measure needs to emanate from policymakers at policy level. A recent large-scale study undertaken in Spain with over 3,800 secondary education students (Lorenzo, Granados, & Rico, 2021) proves that, whereas social class presents a steady impact on non-CLIL students' academic results (students from a higher social class achieving better results), CLIL students obtained equally high results irrespective of their socioeconomic status. Although the causes behind these results are beyond the scope of the study, the authors attribute these results not only to the language regime of bilingual schools, but also to organizational features and ongoing methodological innovations that give rise to quality schooling (409). This disparity of results between secondary and tertiary education sorely needs further research and the good practices employed in secondary education may need to be adopted at university level.

This Element is aimed not only at raising awareness and shedding light on the tools needed to improve EMI at university level, but also at proving the need to carry out further research on its impact on different aspects of university practices, results, and policies. Even bearing in mind that EMI practices vary enormously at geographical (macrolevel), institutional (mesolevel), and classroom (microlevel) levels, the way in which EMI spreads needs to be carefully checked in every country, so that it benefits the whole university community without becoming simply a tool for making profit. In addition, as Block and Khan (2021) emphasize, future studies should try to adopt a truly multidimensional approach by drawing on different and multiple data sources and going beyond questionnaires and interviews. With future research in mind, the ROAD-MAPPING framework proposed by Dafouz and Smit (2020) is well worth mentioning, as this ecological framework provides a powerful research tool to study EMI in multilingual university settings. The effectiveness of the ROAD-MAPPING framework as an analytical tool to examine the different dimensions of EMI has been observed both at the country-level (Bradford and Brown [2017] in Japan; Kuteeva [2019] in Sweden; Sahan [2019] in Turkey) and at the multicountry level (Shao [2019] drew comparisons between China, Japan, and the Netherlands).

I would like to conclude by pointing out that university stakeholders who are able to communicate in English in addition to their other language(s) possess a linguistic repertoire that is a reflection of a multicultural identity. This reality can allay the fears that some members of the university community have that EMI (or Englishization in its derogatory equivalent) may bring about a monocultural identity, provided that the local or vernacular languages are fully supported by the local education authorities. In order to avoid potential conflicts due to EMI implementation, university language policy must be a continuous top-down and bottom-up process in which the specific context is considered and the needs and interests of all university stakeholders are valued, discussed, and articulated. Since EMI is subject to local, national, and global forces, each context needs to be considered in light of the experiences gathered in other settings, but without losing sight of its peculiarities. The literature reviewed in this Element reveals the idiosyncratic nature of EMI, as the different realizations of EMI programs are connected to the social, institutional, and socioeconomic reality in which they are located; but this should not come as a surprise, as education in general and higher education in particular is highly contextualized.

References

Ackerley, K., Guarda, M., & Helm, F. (Eds.) (2017). *Sharing Perspectives on English-Medium Instruction*. Bern: Peter Lang.

Aguilar, M. (2017). Engineering Lecturers' Views on CLIL and EMI. *International Journal of Bilingual Education and Bilingualism*, 20(6), 722–35.

Aguilar, M., & Muñoz, C. (2014). The Effect of Proficiency on CLIL Benefits in Engineering Students in Spain. *International Journal of Applied Linguistics*, 24(1), 1–18.

Airey, J. (2009). *Science, Language and Literacy: Case Studies of Learning in Swedish University Physics*. Uppsala Dissertations from the Faculty of Science and Technology 81. Uppsala: Acta Universitatis Upsaliensis. http://publications.uu.se/theses/abstract.xsql?dbid=9547.

Airey, J. (2012). "I Don't Teach Language": The Linguistic Attitudes of Physics Lecturers in Sweden. *AILA Review*, 25(1), 64–79.

Airey, J. (2015). From Stimulated Recall to Disciplinary Literacy: Summarizing Ten Years of Research into Teaching and Learning in English. In S. Dimova, A. Hultgren, & C. Jensen (Eds.), *English-Medium Instruction in European Higher Education*. Berlin: De Gruyter Mouton, 157–76.

Airey, J. (2020). The Content Lecturer and English-Medium Instruction (EMI): Epilogue to the Special Issue on EMI in Higher Education. *International Journal of Bilingual Education and Bilingualism*, 23(3), 340–46.

Altbach, P., & Knight, J. (2007). The Internationalisation of Higher Education: Motivations and Realities. *Journal of Studies in International Education*, 11 (3–4), 290–305.

Arkın, E., & Osam, N. (2015). English-Medium Higher Education: A Case Study in a Turkish University Context. In S. Dimova, A. K. Hultgren, & C. Jensen (Eds.), *English-Medium Instruction in European Higher Education*. Berlin: De Gruyter Mouton, 177–99.

Arnó-Maciá, E., & Aguilar-Pérez, M. (2021). Language Issues in EMI: When Lecturers and Students Can Choose the Language of Instruction. In D. Block & S. Khan (Eds.), *The Secret Life of English-Medium Instruction in Higher Education. Examining Microphenomena in Context* New York: Routledge, 19–42.

Arnó-Maciá, E., & Mancho-Barés, G. (2015). The Role of Content and Language in Content and Language Integrated Learning (CLIL) at University: Challenges and Implications for ESP. *English for Specific Purposes*, 37, 63–73.

Baker, W., & Hüttner, J. (2017). English and More: A Multisite Study of Roles and Conceptualisations of Language in English Medium Multilingual Universities from Europe to Asia. *Journal of Multilingual and Multicultural Development*, 38(6), 501–16.

Ball, P., & Lindsay, D. (2013). Language Demand and Support for English-Medium Instruction in Tertiary Education. Learning from the Specific Context. In A. Doiz, D. Lasagabaster, & J. M. Sierra (Eds.), *English-Medium Instruction at University: Global Challenges*. Bristol: Multilingual Matters, 44–61.

Banegas, D. L., & Manzur Busleimán, G. (2021). EMI Materials in Online Initial English Language Teaching Education. In D. Lasagabaster, & A. Doiz (Eds.), *Language Use in English-Medium Instruction at University: International Perspectives on Teacher Practice*. New York: Routledge, 100–25.

Banegas, D. L., Poole, P., & Corrales, K. (2020). Content and Language Integrated Learning in Latin America 2008–2018: Ten Years of Research and Practice. *Studies in Second Language Learning & Teaching*, 10(2), 283–305.

Basturkmen, H. (2019). ESP Teacher Education Needs. *Language Teaching*, 52 (3), 318–30.

Belhiah H., & Elhami M. (2015). English as a Medium of Instruction in the Gulf: When Students and Teachers Speak. *Language Policy*, 14(1), 3–23.

Belyaeva, E., Kuznetsova, L., Nikiforova, O., & Suchkova, S. (2021). The Place of English in the Russian Higher Education Landscape. In R. Wilkinson & R. Gabriëls (Eds.), *The Englishisation of Higher Education in Europe*. Amsterdam: Amsterdam University Press, 189–213.

Berry, C., & Taylor, J. (2013). Internationalisation in Higher Education in Latin America: Policies and Practice in Colombia and Mexico. *Higher Education*, 67(5), 585–601.

Block, D. (2021). Emergent STEM Lecturer Identities: The Shaping Effects of EMI in Action in an Internationalised and Englishised HE Context. *Language Teaching*, 54(3), 388–406.

Block, D., & Khan, S. (Eds.) (2021). *The Secret Life of English-Medium Instruction in Higher Education: Examining Microphenomena in Context*. New York: Routledge.

Block, D., & Mancho-Barés, G. (2021). NOT English Teachers, Except When They Are: The Curious Case of Oral Presentation Evaluation Rubrics in an EMI-in-HE Context. In D. Block & S. Khan (Eds.), *The Secret Life of English-Medium Instruction in Higher Education: Examining Microphenomena in Context*. New York: Routledge, 96–119.

Borsetto, E., & Bier, A. (2021). Building on International Good Practices and Experimenting with Different Teaching Methods to Address Local Training Needs: The Academic Lecturing Experience. *Alicante Journal of English Studies*, 34, 107–30.

Bradford, A. (2019). It's Not All about English! The Problem of Language Foregrounding in English-Medium Programmes in Japan. *Journal of Multilingual and Multicultural Development*, 40(8), 707–20.

Bradford, A., & Brown, H. (Eds.) (2017a). *English-Medium Instruction in Japanese Higher Education: Policy, Challenges and Outcomes*. Bristol: Multilingual Matters.

Bradford, A., & Brown, H. (2017b). ROAD-MAPPING English-Medium Instruction in Japan. In A. Bradford & H. Brown (Eds.), *English-Medium Instruction in Japanese Higher Education: Policy, Challenges and Outcomes*. Bristol: Multilingual Matters, 3–13.

Broggini, S., & Costa, F. (2017). A Survey of English-Medium Instruction in Italian Higher Education: An Updated Perspective from 2012 to 2015. *Journal of Immersion and Content-Based Language Education*, 5(2), 238–64.

Byun, K., Chu, H., Kim, M., et al. et al. (2011). English-Medium Teaching in Korean Higher Education: Policy Debates and Reality. *Higher Education*, 62 (4), 431–49.

Chapple, J. (2015). Teaching in English is Not Necessarily the Teaching of English. *International Education Studies*, 8(3), 1–13.

Chostelidou, D., & Griva, E. (2014). Measuring the Effect of Implementing CLIL in Higher Education: An Experimental Research Project. *Procedia – Social and Behavioral Sciences*, 116, 2169–74.

Chou, M.-H. (2018). Speaking Anxiety and Strategy Use for Learning English as a Foreign Language in Full and Partial English-Medium Instruction Contexts. *TESOL Quarterly*, 52(3), 611–33.

Corrales, K. A., Rey, L. A. P., & Escamilla, N. S. (2016). Is EMI Enough? Perceptions from University Professors and Students. *Latin American Journal of Content & Language Integrated Learning*, 9(2), 318–44.

Costa, F. (2012). Focus on Form in ICLHE Lectures in Italy: Evidence from English-Medium Science Lectures by Native Speakers of Italian. *AILA Review*, 25, 30–47.

Costa, F., & Coleman, J. A. (2013). A Survey of English-Medium Instruction in Italian Higher Education. *International Journal of Bilingual Education and Bilingualism*, 16(1), 3–19.

Curle, S., Yuksel, D., Soruc, A., & Altay, M. (2020). Predictors of English Medium Instruction Academic Success: English Proficiency versus First

Language Medium. *System*, 95, 102378. https://doi.org/10.1016/j.system.2020
.102378.

Dafouz, E. (2018). English-Medium Instruction and Teacher Education Programmes in Higher Education: Ideological Forces and Imagined Identities at Work. *International Journal of Bilingual Education and Bilingualism*, 21(5), 540–52.

Dafouz, E. (2021). Crossing Disciplinary Boundaries: English-Medium Education (EME) Meets English for Specific Purposes (ESP). *Ibérica*, 41, 13–38.

Dafouz, E., & Smit, U. (2020). *Road-Mapping English Medium Education in the Internationalised University*. Cham: Palgrave Pivot.

Dafouz, E., Camacho, M., & Urquia, E. (2014). "Surely They Can't Do as Well": A Comparison of Business Students' Academic Performance in English-Medium and Spanish-as-First-Language-Medium Programmes. *Language and Education*, 28, 223–36.

Dafouz, E., Hüttner, J., & Smit, U. (2016). University Teachers' Beliefs on Language and Content Integration in English-Medium Education in Multilingual Settings. In T. Nikula, E. Dafouz, P. Moore, & U. Smit (Eds.), *Conceptualising Integration in CLIL and Multilingual Education*. Bristol: Multilingual Matters, 123–43.

Dang, T. K. A., Bonar, G. & Yao, J. (2021). Professional Learning for Educators Teaching in English-Medium-Instruction in Higher Education: A Systematic Review. *Teaching in Higher Education*. https://doi.org/10.1080/13562517 .2020.1863350.

Darquennes, J., Du Plessis, T., & Soler, J. (Eds.) (2020). Language Diversity Management in Higher Education. *Sociolinguistica*, 34(1), 1–237.

Dearden, J. (2015). *English as a Medium of Instruction – A Growing Global Phenomenon*. London: British Council. www.britishcouncil.es/sites/default/ files/british_council_english_as_a_medium_of_instruction.pdf

Dimova, S., & Kling, J. (2018). Assessing English-Medium Instruction Lecturer Proficiency across Disciplines. *TESOL Quarterly*, 52(3), 634–56.

Doiz, A., & Lasagabaster, D. (2017). Teachers' Beliefs About Translanguaging Practices. In C. M. Mazak & K. S. Carroll (Eds.), *Translanguaging in Higher Education: Beyond Monolingual Ideologies*. Bristol, England: Multilingual Matters, 157–76.

Doiz, A., & Lasagabaster, D. (2018). Teachers' and Students' L2 Motivational Self-System in English-Medium Instruction: A Qualitative Approach. *TESOL Quarterly*, 52(3), 657–79.

Doiz, A., & Lasagabaster, D. (2020). Dealing with Language Issues in English-Medium Instruction at University: A Comprehensive Approach.

International Journal of Bilingual Education and Bilingualism, 23(3), 257–62.

Doiz, A., & Lasagabaster, D. (2021). Analysing EMI Teachers' and Students' Talk About Language and Language Use. In D. Lasagabaster & A. Doiz (Eds.), *Language Use in English-Medium Instruction at University: International Perspectives on Teacher Practice*. New York: Routledge, 34–55.

Doiz, A., & Lasagabaster, D., & Pavón, V. (2019). The Integration of Language and Content in English-Medium Instruction Courses: Lecturers' Beliefs and Practices. *Ibérica*, 38, 151–75.

Doiz, A., Lasagabaster, D., & Sierra, J. M. (Eds.) (2013a). *English-Medium Instruction at Universities: Global Challenges*. Bristol: Multilingual Matters.

Doiz, A., Lasagabaster, D., & Sierra, J. (2013b). Globalisation, Internationalisation, Multilingualism and Linguistic Strains in Higher Education. *Studies in Higher Education*, 38(9), 1407–21.

Doiz, A., Lasagabaster, D., & Sierra, J. (2014). Language Friction and Multilingual Policies at Higher Education: The Stakeholders' View. *Journal of Multilingual and Multicultural Development*, 35(4), 345–60.

Drljača Margić, B., & Vodopija-Krstanović, I. (2018). Language Development for English-Medium Instruction: Teachers' Perceptions, Reflections and Learning. *Journal of English for Academic Purposes*, 35, 31–41.

Dubow, G., & Gundermann, S. (2017). Certifying the Linguistic and Communicative Competencies of Teachers in English-Medium Instruction Programmes. *Language Learning in Higher Education*, 7(2), 475–87.

Elliott, N., Vila, F. X., & Gilabert, R. (2018). The Presentation of Catalan Universities: Linguistic Reality to a Transnational Audience. *European Journal of Language Policy*, 10(1), 121–46.

Engin, M. (2017). Contributions and Silence in Academic Talk: Exploring Learner Experiences of Dialogic Interaction. *Learning, Culture and Social Interaction*, 12, 78–86.

Evans, S., & Morrison, B. (2011a). Meeting the Challenges of English-Medium Higher Education: The First-Year Experience in Hong Kong. *English for Specific Purposes*, 30, 198–208.

Evans, S., & Morrison, B. (2011b). The Student Experience in English-Medium Higher Education in Hong Kong. *Language and Education*, 25(2), 147–62.

Farrell, T. S. C. (2020). Professional Development Through Reflective Practice for English-Medium Instruction (EMI) Teachers. *International Journal of Bilingual Education and Bilingualism*, 23(3), 277–86.

Fortanet-Gómez, I. (2013). *CLIL in Higher Education: Towards a Multilingual Language Policy*. Bristol: Multilingual Matters.

Fortanet-Gómez, I. (2020). The Dimensions of EMI in the International Classroom: Training Teachers for the Future University. In M. M. Sánchez-Pérez (Ed.), *Teacher Training for English-Medium Instruction in Higher Education*. Hershey, PA: IGI Global, 1–20.

Galloway, N., Kriukow, J. & Numajiri, T. (2017). *Internationalisation, Higher Education and the Growing Demand for English: An Investigation into the English Medium Instruction (EMI) Movement in China and Japan*. London: British Council.

Gill, S. K., & Kirkpatrick, A. (2013). English in Asian and European Higher Education. In C. A. Chapelle (Ed.), *The Encyclopedia of Applied Linguistics*. London: Blackwell, 1–4.

Gimenez, T., Sarmento, S., Archanjo, R., Zicman, R., & Finardi, K. (2018). *Guide to English as a Medium of Instruction in Brazilian Higher Education Institutions (2018–2019)*. London: British Council. www.britishcouncil.org.br/sites/default/files/guide_to_english_as_medium_of_instruction_2018-19.pdf.

Graham, K. M., Eslami, Z. R., & Hillman, S. (2021). From English as the Medium to English as a Medium: Perspectives of EMI students in Qatar. *System*, 99, 102508.

Gregersen, F. et al. (2018). *More Parallel, Please! Best Practice of Parallel Language Use at Nordic Universities: 11 Recommendations*. Denmark: Nordic Council of Ministers. https://norden.diva-portal.org/smash/get/diva2:1203291/FULLTEXT01.pdf.

Guarda, M., & Helm, F. (2017a). A Survey of Lecturers' Needs and Feedback on EMI Training. In K. Ackerley, M. Guarda, & F. Helm (Eds.), *Sharing Perspectives on English-Medium Instruction*. Bern: Peter Lang, 167–94.

Guarda, M., & Helm, F. (2017b). "I Have Discovered New Teaching Pathways": The Link Between Language Shift and Teaching Practice. *International Journal of Bilingual Education and Bilingualism*, 20(7), 897–913.

Haberland, H. (2014). English from Above and Below, and from Outside. In A. K. Hultgren, F. Gregersen, & J. Thøgersen (Eds.), *English in Nordic Universities: Ideologies and Practices*. Amsterdam: John Benjamins, 251–63.

Haberland, H., & Preisler, B. (2015). The Position of Danish, English and Other Languages at Danish Universities in the Context of Danish Society. In F. X. Vila & V. Bretxa (Eds.), *Language Policy in Higher Education: The Case of Medium-Sized Languages*. Bristol: Multilingual Matters, 15–42.

Hamel, R. E., Álvarez López, E., & Pereira Carvalhal, T. (2016). Language Policy and Planning: Challenges for Latin American Universities. *Current Issues in Language Planning*, 17(3/4), 278–97.

Haugen, E. (1971). *The Ecology of Language*. Report 13. Washington, DC: Center for Applied Linguistics.

Helm, F., & Guarda, M. (2015). "Improvisation is Not Allowed in a Second Language": A Survey of Italian Lecturers' Concerns about Teaching Their Subjects through English. *Language Learning in Higher Education*, 5(2), 353–73.

Henriksen, B., Holmen, A., & Kling, J. (2019). *English Medium Instruction in Multilingual and Multicultural Universities: Academics Voices from the Northern European Context*. New York: Routledge.

Hernández-Nanclares, N., & Jiménez-Muñoz, A. (2017). English as a Medium of Instruction: Evidence for Language and Content Targets in Bilingual Education in Economics. *International Journal of Bilingual Education and Bilingualism*, 20(7), 883–96.

Hibbert, L., & van der Walt, C. (Eds.) (2014). *Multilingual Universities in South Africa: Reflecting Society in Higher Education*. Bristol: Multilingual Matters.

Hu, G., & Lei, J. (2014). English-Medium Instruction in Chinese Higher Education: A Case Study. *Higher Education*, 67(5), 551–67.

Hu, J. & Wu, P. (2020). Understanding English Language Learning in Tertiary English Medium Instruction Contexts in China. *System*, 93, 102305.

Hultgren, A. K., Owen, N., Shrestha, P., Kuteeva, M., & Mezek, S. (2022). Assessment and English as a Medium of Instruction: Challenges and Opportunities. *Journal of English-Medium Instruction*, 1(1), 105–123.

Inbar-Lourie, O., & Donitsa-Schmidt, S. (2020). EMI Lecturers in International Universities: is a Native/Non-Native English-Speaking Background Relevant? *International Journal of Bilingual Education and Bilingualism*, 23(3), 301–13.

Järlström, M., Piekkari, R., Pilke, N., & Turpeinen, H. (2020). Perceptions of Language (Mis)Fit at a Multilingual Workplace: The Case of the University of Vaasa. In M. Kuteeva, Kaufhold, K., & Hynninen, N. (Eds.), *Language Perceptions and Practices in Multilingual Universities*. Cham: Palgrave Macmillan, 293–322.

Jaspers, J. (2018). The Transformative Limits of Translanguaging. *Language and Communication*, 58, 1–10.

Jiang, L., Zhang, L. J., & May, S. (2019). Implementing English-Medium Instruction (EMI) in China: Teachers' Practices and Perceptions, and Students' Learning Motivation and Needs. *International Journal of Bilingual Education and Bilingualism*, 22(2), 107–19.

Joe, Y. & H.-K. Lee (2013). Does English-Medium Instruction Benefit Students in EFL Contexts? A Case Study of Medical Students in Korea. *Asia-Pacific Education Research*, 22(2), 201–7.

Kachru, B. B. (Ed.) (1992). *The Other Tongue: English across Cultures*, 2nd ed. Urbana: University of Illinois Press.

Kamasak, R., Hasan, K., & Rose, H. (2021). Academic Language-Related Challenges at an English-Medium University. *Journal of English for Academic Purposes*, 49, 100945.

Kim, E. G. (2017). English Medium Instruction in Korean Higher Education: Challenges and Future Directions. In B. Fenton-Smith, P. Humphreys, & I. Walkinshaw (Eds.), *English Medium Instruction in Higher Education in Asia-Pacific*. Multilingual Education, vol. 21. Cham: Springer, 53–69.

Kim, J., Kim, E. G., & Kweon, S. (2018). Challenges in Implementing English-Medium Instruction: Perspectives of Humanities and Social Sciences Professors Teaching Engineering Students. *English for Specific Purposes*, 51, 111–23.

Kim E. G., & Yoon J.-R. (2018). Korean Science and Engineering Students' Perceptions of English-Medium Instruction and Korean-Medium Instruction. *Journal of Language Identity & Education*, 17(3), 182–97.

Kirkpatrick, A. (2011a). English as an Asian Lingua Franca and the Multilingual Model of ELT. *Language Teaching*, 44(2), 212–24.

Kirkpatrick, A. (2011b). English as a Medium of Instruction in Asian Education (from Primary to Tertiary): Implications for Local Languages and Local Scholarship. *Applied Linguistics Review*, 2, 99–120.

Konakahara, M., Murata, K., & Iino, M. (2019). English-Medium Instruction in a Japanese University: Exploring Students' and Lecturers' Voices from an ELF Perspective. In K. Murata (Ed.), *English-Medium Instruction from an English as a Lingua Franca Perspective: Exploring the Higher Education Context*. New York: Routledge, 157–75.

Kuteeva, M. (Ed.) (2011). Special Issue on Academic English in Parallel-Language and ELF Settings. *Ibérica*, 22, 1–162.

Kuteeva, M. (2019). Researching English-Medium Instruction at Swedish Universities: Developments Over the Past Decade. In K. Murata (Ed.), *English-Medium Instruction from an English as a Lingua Franca Perspective*. Abingdon: Routledge, 46–63.

Kuteeva, M. (2020). Revisiting the 'E' in EMI: Students' Perceptions of Standard English, Lingua Franca and Translingual Practices. *International Journal of Bilingual Education and Bilingualism*, 23(3), 287–300.

Kuteeva, M., & Airey, J. (2014). Disciplinary Differences in the Use of English in Higher Education: Reflections on Recent Language Policy Developments. *Higher Education*, 67, 533–49.

Kuteeva, M., Kaufhold, K., & Hynninen, N. (Eds.) (2020). *Language Perceptions and Practices in Multilingual Universities*. Cham: Palgrave Macmillan.

Lanvers, U., & Hultgren, A. K. (2018). The Englishisation of European education: Concluding Remarks. *European Journal of Language Policy*, 10(1), 147–52.

Lasagabaster, D. (2018). Fostering Team Teaching: Mapping Out a Research Agenda for English-Medium Instruction at University Level. *Language Teaching*, 51(3), 400–16.

Lasagabaster, D. (2021a). Team Teaching: A Way to Boost the Quality of EMI Programmes? In F. Rubio-Alcalá & D. Coyle (Eds.), *Developing and Evaluating Quality Bilingual Practices in Higher Education*. Bristol: Multilingual Matters, 163–80.

Lasagabaster, D. (2021b). Striving to Maintain a Multilingual Balance. In R. Wilkinson & R. Gabriëls (Eds.), *The Englishisation of Higher Education in Europe*. Amsterdam: Amsterdam University Press, 77–95.

Lasagabaster, D. (2022). Teacher Preparedness for English-Medium Instruction. *Journal of English-Medium Instruction*, 1(1), 48–64.

Lasagabaster, D., & Doiz, A. (Eds.) (2021). *Language Use in English-Medium Instruction at University: International Perspectives on Teacher Practice*. New York: Routledge.

Lasagabaster, D., Doiz, A., Pavón, V. (2018). Undergraduates' Beliefs about the Role of Language and Team Teaching in EMI Courses at University. *Rassegna Italiana di Linguistica Applicata*, 2–3, 111–27.

Lawrence, C., Inbar-Lourie, O., & Weinberg, L. (2017). *A Handbook for English-Medium Instruction in Institutions of Higher Education in Israel: English as the Cornerstone of Sustainable Technology and Research*. Tel Aviv: University of Tel Aviv.

Lei, J., & Hu, G. (2014). Is English-Medium Instruction Effective in Improving Chinese Undergraduate Students' English Competence? *International Review of Applied Linguistics in Language Teaching*, 52(2), 99–126.

Liddicoat, A. J. (Ed.) (2018). *Language Policy and Planning in Universities: Teaching, Research and Administration*. New York: Routledge.

Lin, A. M. Y. (2016). *Language across the Curriculum & CLIL in English as an Additional Language (EAL) Contexts: Theory and Practice*. Singapore: Springer.

Llanes, À., & Cots, J. M. (2020). Measuring the Impact of Translanguaging In TESOL: A Plurilingual Approach to ESP. *International Journal of Multilingualism*. https://doi.org/10.1080/14790718.2020.1753749.

Llurda, E., Cots, J. M., & Armengol, L. (2014). Views on Multilingualism and Internationalisation in Higher Education: Administrative Staff in the

Spotlight. *Journal of Multilingual and Multicultural Development*, 35(4), 376–91.

Lorenzo, F., Granados, A., & Rico, N. (2021). Equity in Bilingual Education: Socioeconomic Status and Content and Language Integrated Learning in Monolingual Southern Europe. *Applied Linguistics*, 42(3), 393–413.

Luckett, K., & Hurst-Harosh, E. (2021). Translanguaging Pedagogies in the Humanities and Social Sciences in South Africa: Affordances and Constraints. In B. A. Paulsrud, Z. Tian, & J. Toth (Eds.), *English-Medium Instruction and Translanguaging*. Bristol: Multilingual Matters.

Lueg, K., & Lueg, R. (2015). Why Do Students Choose English as a Medium of Instruction? A Bourdieusian Perspective on the Study Strategies of Non-Native English Speakers. *Academy of Management Learning and Education*, 14(1), 5–30.

Macaro, E. (2018). *English Medium Instruction: Content and Language in Policy and Practice*. Oxford: Oxford University Press.

Macaro, E., & Han, S. (2020). English Medium Instruction in China's Higher Education: Teachers' Perspectives of Competencies, Certification and Professional Development. *Journal of Multilingual and Multicultural Development*, 41, 219–31.

Macaro, E., Jiménez-Muñoz, J. A., & Lasagabaster, D. (2019). The Importance of Certification of English Medium Instruction Teachers in Higher Education in Spain. *Porta Linguarum*, 32, 103–18.

Macaro, E., Curle, S., Pun, J., An, J., & Dearden, J. (2018). A Systematic Review of English Medium Instruction in Higher Education. *Language Teaching*, 51(1), 36–76.

Malmström, H., & Pecorari, D. (2021). Epilogue: Disciplinary Literacies as a Nexus for Content and Language Teacher Practice. In D. Lasagabaster & A. Doiz (Eds.), *Language Use in English-Medium Instruction at University: International Perspectives on Teacher Practice*. New York: Routledge, 213–21.

Malmström, H., Pecorari, D., & Gustafsson, M. (2016). Size and Development of Academic Vocabulary in English Medium Instruction. In S. Göpferich, & I. Neumann (Eds.), *Developing and Assessing Academic and Professional Writing Skills*. Bern: Peter Lang, 45–69.

Mancho-Barés. G., & Aguilar-Pérez, M. (2020). EMI Lecturers' Practices in Correcting English: Resources for Language Teaching? *Journal of Immersion and Content-Based Language Teaching*, 8(2), 257–84.

Marcos-García, A. M., & Pavón, V. (2018). The Linguistic Internationalisation of Higher Education: A Study on the Presence of Language Policies and Bilingual Studies in Spanish Universities. *Porta Linguarum*, 3, 31–46.

Martinez, R. (2016). English as a Medium of Instruction (EMI) in Brazilian Higher Education: Challenges and Opportunities. In K. R. Finardi (Ed.), *English in Brazil: Views, Policies and Programs*. Londrina: SciELO-EDUEL, 191–228.

Martinez, R., Machado, P., & Palma, C. (2021). An Exploratory Analysis of Language-Related Episodes (LREs) in a Brazilian EMI Context: Lecturers' and Students' Perspectives. In Mazak, C. M., & Carroll, K. S. (Eds.), *Translanguaging in Higher Education: Beyond Monolingual Ideologies*. Bristol: Multilingual Matters.

Morell, T. (2020). EMI Teacher Training with a Multimodal and Interactive Approach: A New Horizon for LSP Specialists. *Language Value*, 12(1), 56–87.

Motta, A. (2017). Nine and a Half Reasons against the Monarchy of English. In K. Ackerley, M. Guarda & F. Helm (Eds.), *Sharing Perspectives on English-Medium Instruction*. Bern: Peter Lang, 95–110.

Muguruza, B., Cenoz, J., & Gorter, D. (2020). Implementing Translanguaging Pedagogies in an English Medium Instruction Course. *International Journal of Multilingualism*, 1–16.

Murata, K. (Ed.) (2019). *English-Medium Instruction from an English as a Lingua Franca Perspective: Exploring the Higher Education Context*. New York: Routledge.

Núñez Asomoza, A. (2015). Students' Perceptions of the Impact of CLIL in a Mexican BA Program. *PROFILE Issues in Teachers' Professional Development*, 17(2), 111–24.

O'Dowd, R. (2018). The Training and Accreditation of Teachers for English Medium Instruction: An Overview of Practice in European Universities. *International Journal of Bilingual Education and Bilingualism*, 21(5), 553–63.

Orduna-Nocito, E., & Sánchez-García, D. (2021). Aligning Higher Education Language Policies with Lecturers' Views on EMI Practices: A Comparative Study of Ten European Universities. *System*, 104, 102692.

Pagèze, J., & Lasagabaster, D. (2017). Teacher Development for Teaching and Learning in English in a French Higher Education Context. *L'Analisi Linguistica E Letteraria*, 25, 289–310.

Paulsrud, B. A., Tian, Z., & Toth, J. (Eds.) (2021). *English-Medium Instruction and Translanguaging*. Bristol: Multilingual Matters.

Pecorari, D., & Halmström, H. (2018a). At the Crossroads of TESOL and English Medium Instruction. *TESOL Quarterly*, 52(3), 497–515.

Pecorari, D., & Halmström, H. (Eds.) (2018b). At the Crossroads of TESOL and English Medium Instruction. *TESOL Quarterly*, 52(3), 493–720.

Peng, J.-E, & Xie, X. (2021). English-Medium Instruction as a Pedagogical Strategy for the Sustainable Development of EFL Learners in the Chinese Context: A Meta-Analysis of Its Effectiveness. *Sustainability*, 13, 5637.

Phillipson, R. (2006). English, a Cuckoo in the European Higher Education Nest of Languages? *European Journal of English Studies*, 10(1), 13–32.

Pompeu Fabra University (2007). *The Plan of Action for Multilingualism*. Barcelona: Pompeu Fabra University. www.upf.edu/documents/225732635/226180811/PAM/01c4da27-15b8-9bb9-85a6-a31f5de126f9.

Pulcini, V., & Campagna, S. (2015). Internationalisation and the EMI Controversy in Italian Higher Education. In S. Dimova, A. K. Hultgren, & C. Jensen (Eds.), *English-Medium Instruction in European Higher Education*. Berlin: De Gruyter Mouton, 65–87.

Reilly, C. (2021). Malawian Universities as Translanguaging Spaces. In B. A. Paulsrud, Z. Tian, & J. Toth (Eds.), *English-Medium Instruction and Translanguaging*. Bristol: Multilingual Matters, 29–42.

Richter, K. (2019). *English-Medium Instruction and Pronunciation: Exposure and Skills Development*. Bristol: Multilingual Matters.

Risager, K. (2012). Language Hierarchies at the International University. *International Journal of the Sociology of Language*, 216, 111–30.

Rogier, D. (2012). The Effects of English-Medium Instruction on Language Proficiency of Students Enrolled in Higher Education in the UAE. PhD dissertation. University of Exeter. https://ore.exeter.ac.uk/repository/bitstream/handle/10036/4482/RogierD.pdf?sequence=2.

Roothooft, H. (2022). Spanish Lecturers' Beliefs about English Medium Instruction: STEM Versus Humanities. *International Journal of Bilingual Education and Bilingualism*, 25(2), 627–40.

Rose, H. (2021). Students' Language-Related Challenges of Studying through English: What EMI Teachers Can Do. In D. Lasagabaster & A. Doiz (Eds.), *Language Use in English-Medium Instruction at University: International Perspectives on Teacher Practice*. New York: Routledge, 145–66.

Rose, H., & Galloway, N. (2019). *Global Englishes for Language Teaching*. Cambridge: Cambridge University Press.

Rose, H., & McKinley, J. (2018). Japan's English-Medium Instruction Initiatives and the Globalization of Higher Education. *Higher Education*, 75(1), 111–29.

Rose, H., Curle, S., Aizawa, I., & Thompson, G. (2020). What Drives Success in English Medium Taught Courses? The Interplay Between Language Proficiency, Academic Skills, and Motivation. *Studies in Higher Education*, 45(11), 2149–61.

Rubio-Alcalá, F., & Coyle, D. (2021). *Developing and Evaluating Quality Bilingual Practices in Higher Education*. Bristol: Multilingual Matters.

Rubio-Alcalá, F., & Mallorquín, S. (2020). Teacher Training Competences and Subsequent Training Design for Higher Education Plurilingual Programs. In M. M. Sánchez-Pérez (Ed.), *Teacher Training for English-Medium Instruction in Higher Education*. Hershey, PA: IGI Global, 41–61

Ruiz De Zarobe, Y., & Lyster, R. (Eds.) (2018). Content and Language Integration in Higher Education: Instructional Practices and Teacher Development. *International Journal of Bilingual Education and Bilingualism* (Special Issue), 21(5), 523–615.

Ryan, J. (2018). Voices from the Field: Email Interviews with Applied Linguists in Asia. In R.Barnard & Z. Hasim (Eds.), *English Medium Instruction Programmes: Perspectives from South East Asian Universities*. New York: Routledge, 15–28.

Saarinen, T. (2012). Internationalisation of Finnish Higher Education – Is Language an Issue? *International Journal of the Sociology of Language*, 216, 157–73.

Sahan, K. (2019). Variations of the English-Medium Instruction: Comparing Policy and Practice in Turkish Higher Education. Unpublished doctoral dissertation. University of Oxford.

Sahan, K., Rose, H., & Macaro, E. (2021). Models of EMI Pedagogies: At the Interface of Language Use and Interaction. *System*, 101, 102616.

Sahan, K., Mikoljewska, A., Rose, H., et al. (2021). *Global Mapping of English as a Medium of Instruction in Higher Education: 2020 and Beyond*. London: British Council.

Sánchez-García, D. (2020). Mapping Lecture Questions and Their Pedagogical Goals in Spanish- and English-Medium Instruction. *Journal of Immersion and Content-Based Language Education*, 8(1), 28–52.

Sánchez-Pérez, M. M. (2020). *Teacher Training for English-Medium Instruction in Higher Education*. Hershey, PA: IGI Global.

Sánchez-Pérez, M. M. (2021). Predicting Content Proficiency through Disciplinary-Literacy Variables in English-Medium Writing. *System*, 97, 102463.

Schmidt-Unterberger, B. (2018). The English-Medium Paradigm: A Conceptualization of English-Medium Teaching in Higher Education. *International Journal of Bilingual Education and Bilingualism*, 21(5), 527–39.

Shagrir, L. (2017). Collaborating with Colleagues for the Sake of Academic and Professional Development in Higher Education. *International Journal for Academic Development*, 22(4), 331–42.

Shao, L. (2019). Case Studies of English-Medium Instruction in Higher Education: Business Programmes in China, Japan and the Netherlands. Unpublished doctoral dissertation. University of Dublin, Trinity College, Ireland. www.tara.tcd.ie/bitstream/handle/2262/88792/Final-E-Thesis%20upload-with-%20transcripts-final%20submission-Lijie-thesis-.pdf.

Shohamy, E. (2013). A Critical Perspective on the Use of English as a Medium of Instruction at Universities. In A. Doiz, D. Lasagabaster & J. M. Sierra (Eds.), *English-Medium Instruction at Universities: Global Challenges*. Bristol: Multilingual Matters, 196–221.

Smit, U. (2010). *English as a Lingua Franca in Higher Education: A Longitudinal Study of Classroom Discourse*. Berlin: Mouton De Gruyter.

Söderlundh, H. (2013). Applying Transnational Strategies Locally: English as a Medium of Instruction in Swedish Higher Education. *Nordic Journal of English Studies*, 13(1), 113–32.

Song, M.-M., & Tai, H. H. (2007). Taiwan's Responses to Globalisation: Internationalisation and Questing for World Class Universities. *Asia Pacific Journal of Education*, 27(3), 323–40.

Tatzl, D., & Messnarz, B. (2013). Testing Foreign Language Impact on Engineering Students' Scientific Problem-Solving Performance. *European Journal of Engineering Education*, 38(6), 620–30.

Tedick, D. J., & Cammarata, L. (2012). Content and Language Integration in K-12 Contexts: Student Outcomes, Teacher Practices, and Stakeholder Perspectives. *Foreign Language Annals*, 45(1), 28–53.

Tejada-Sánchez, I., & Molina-Naar, M. (2020). English Medium Instruction and the Internationalisation of Higher Education in Latin America: A Case Study from a Colombian University. *Latin American Journal of Content & Language Integrated Learning*, 13(2), 339–67.

Tsou, W. (2017). Interactional Skills in Engineering Education. In W. Tsou & S.-M. Kao (Eds.), *English as a Medium of Instruction in Higher Education: Implementations and Classroom Practices in Taiwan*. New York: Springer, 79–93.

Thøgersen, J., & Airey, J. (2011). Lecturing Undergraduate Science in Danish and in English: A Comparison of Speaking Rate and Rhetorical Style. *English for Specific Purposes*, 30(3), 209–21.

Tuomainen, S. (2018). Supporting Non-Native University Lecturers with English-Medium Instruction. *Journal of Applied Research in Higher Education*, 10(3), 230–42.

Valcke, J., & Wilkinson, R. (Eds.) (2017). *Integrating Content and Language in Higher Education: Perspectives on Professional Practice*. Frankfurt am Main: Peter Lang.

van der Walt, Christa. (2013). *Multilingual Higher Education: Beyond English Medium Orientations*. Bristol: Multilingual Matters.

Van Parijs, P. (2011). *Linguistic Justice for Europe and for the World*. Oxford: Oxford University Press.

Vila, F. X., & Bretxa, V. (Eds.). (2015). *Language Policy in Higher Education: The Case of Medium-Sized Languages*. Bristol: Multilingual Matters.

Wächter, B., & Maiworm, F. (Eds.). (2014). *English-Taught Programmes in European Higher Education: The State of Play in 2014*. Bonn: Lemmens.

Weimberg, L., & Symon, M. (2017). Crossing Borders: The Challenges and Benefits of a Collaborative Approach to Course Development Involving Content and Language Specialists in Different Countries. In J. Valcke & R. Wilkinson (Eds.), *Integrating Content and Language in Higher Education: Perspectives and Professional Practice*. Frankfurt am Main: Peter Lang, 135–50.

Werther, C., Denver, L., Jensen, C., & Mees, I. M. (2014). Using English as a Medium of Instruction at University Level in Denmark: The Lecturer's Perspective. *Journal of Multilingual and Multicultural Development*, 35(5), 443–62.

Wilkinson, R. (2013). English-Medium Instruction at a Dutch University: Challenges and Pitfalls. In A. Doiz, D. Lasagabaster, & J. M. Sierra (Eds.), *English-Medium Instruction at Universities: Global Challenges*. Bristol: Multilingual Matters, 3–24.

Wilkinson, R. (2017). Trends and Issues in English-Medium Instruction in Europe. In K. Ackerley, M. Guarda, & F. Helm (Eds.), *Sharing Perspectives on English-Medium Instruction*. Bern: Peter Lang, 35–75.

Wilkinson, R., & Gabriëls, R. (Eds.) (2021). *The Englishisation of Higher Education in Europe*. Amsterdam: Amsterdam University Press.

Wilkinson, R., & Walsh, M. L. (Eds.) (2015). *Integrating Content and Language in Higher Education: From Theory to Practice*. Frankfurt am Main: Peter Lang.

Xie, W., & Curle, S. (2019). Success in English Medium Instruction in China: Significant Indicators and Implications. *International Journal of Bilingual Education and Bilingualism*. https://doi.org/10.1080/13670050.2019.1703898.

Yang, W. (2015). Content and Language Integrated Learning Next in Asia: Evidence of Learners' Achievement in CLIL Education from a Taiwan Tertiary Degree Programme. *International Journal of Bilingual Education and Bilingualism*, 18(4), 361–82.

Zhang, L. (2017). Classroom Discourse in Content-Based Instruction in Higher Education: A Focus on Teachers' Use of Metadiscourse. Unpublished PhD dissertation. University of Hong Kong.

Acknowledgments

The author would like to thank the editors, Heath Rose and Jim McKinley, for their invitation to write this Element. I am also grateful to the reviewers for their careful reading of the manuscript and their insightful comments. All remaining shortcomings are my own. This work is part of the following research projects: PID2020-117882GB-I00 (Spanish Ministry of Science and Innovation) and IT1426-22 (Department of Education, Basque Government).

Cambridge Elements ≡

Elements in Language Teaching

Heath Rose

Linacre College, University of Oxford

Heath Rose is an Associate Professor of Applied Linguistics at the University of Oxford. At Oxford, he is course director of the MSc in Applied Linguistics for Language Teaching. Before moving into academia, Heath worked as a language teacher in Australia and Japan in both school and university contexts. He is author of numerous books, such as *Introducing Global Englishes, The Japanese Writing System, Data Collection Research Methods in Applied Linguistics*, and *Global Englishes for Language Teaching*. Heath's research interests are firmly situated within the field of second language teaching, and includes work on Global Englishes, teaching English as an international language, and English Medium Instruction.

Jim McKinley

University College London

Jim McKinley is an Associate Professor of Applied Linguistics and TESOL at UCL, Institute of Education, where he serves as Academic Head of Learning and Teaching. His major research areas are second language writing in global contexts, the internationalisation of higher education, and the relationship between teaching and research. Jim has edited or authored numerous books including the *Routledge Handbook of Research Methods in Applied Linguistics, Data Collection Research Methods in Applied Linguistics*, and *Doing Research in Applied Linguistics*. He is also an editor of the journal *System*. Before moving into academia, Jim taught in a range of diverse contexts including the US, Australia, Japan, and Uganda.

Advisory Board

Brian Paltridge, *University of Sydney*
Gary Barkhuizen, *University of Auckland*
Marta Gonzalez-Lloret, *University of Hawaii*
Li Wei, *UCL Institute of Education*
Victoria Murphy, *University of Oxford*
Diane Pecorari, *City University of Hong Kong*
Christa Van der *Walt, Stellenbosch University*

About the Series

This Elements series aims to close the gap between researchers and practitioners by allying research with language teaching practices, in its exploration of research-informed teaching, and teaching-informed research. The series builds upon a rich history of pedagogical research in its exploration of new insights within the field of language teaching.

Cambridge Elements $^{\equiv}$

Elements in Language Teaching

Printed in the United States
by Baker & Taylor Publisher Services

T0311588

Cambridge Elements ≡

Elements in Musical Theatre
edited by
William A. Everett
University of Missouri-Kansas City

"WHY AREN'T THEY TALKING?"

The Sung-Through Musical from the 1980s to the 2010s

Alex Bádue

CAMBRIDGE
UNIVERSITY PRESS

CAMBRIDGE
UNIVERSITY PRESS

University Printing House, Cambridge CB2 8BS, United Kingdom

One Liberty Plaza, 20th Floor, New York, NY 10006, USA

477 Williamstown Road, Port Melbourne, VIC 3207, Australia

314–321, 3rd Floor, Plot 3, Splendor Forum, Jasola District Centre, New Delhi – 110025, India

103 Penang Road, #05–06/07, Visioncrest Commercial, Singapore 238467

Cambridge University Press is part of the University of Cambridge.

It furthers the University's mission by disseminating knowledge in the pursuit of education, learning, and research at the highest international levels of excellence.

www.cambridge.org
Information on this title: www.cambridge.org/9781108791939
DOI: 10.1017/9781108866866

© Alex Bádue 2022

This publication is in copyright. Subject to statutory exception and to the provisions of relevant collective licensing agreements, no reproduction of any part may take place without the written permission of Cambridge University Press.

First published 2022

A catalogue record for this publication is available from the British Library.

ISBN 978-1-108-79193-9 Paperback
ISSN 2631-6528 (online)
ISSN 2631-651X (print)

Cambridge University Press has no responsibility for the persistence or accuracy of URLs for external or third-party internet websites referred to in this publication and does not guarantee that any content on such websites is, or will remain, accurate or appropriate.

"Why Aren't They Talking?"

The Sung-Through Musical from the 1980s to the 2010s

Elements in Musical Theatre

DOI: 10.1017/9781108866866
First published online: February 2022

Alex Bádue
Author for correspondence: Alex Bádue, baduealex@gmail.com

Abstract: In the American musical theater, the most typical form of structuring musicals has been the book musical, in which songs interrupt spoken dialogue and add means to depict characters and dramatic situations. After 1980, a form of structuring musicals that expands upon the aesthetic conventions of the book musical came to prominence. Sung-through musicals challenged the balance between talking and singing in musical theater in scripts that are entirely, or nearly entirely, sung. Although often associated with British musicals, this Element focuses on American sung-through musicals composed and premiered between 1980 and 2019. Their creative teams employed specific procedures and compositional techniques through which music establishes characterization and expression when either very little or nothing is spoken and thus define how the musical reinvented itself toward and in the twenty-first century.

Keywords: musical theater, American musical, Broadway musicals, popular music, sung-through musicals

© Alex Bádue 2022

ISBNs: 9781108791939 (PB), 9781108866866 (OC)
ISSNs: 2631-6528 (online), 2631-651X (print)

Contents

1 Introduction

In the 2015 Broadway musical *Something Rotten!* the protagonist, Nick Bottom, desperately seeks to know what the future of Western theater will be so that he can beat his rival, William Shakespeare, in creating the next theatrical success in London of the 1590s. Bottom looks to Thomas Nostradamus, supposed nephew of the legendary sixteenth-century seer, who informs him that theater history will go through extraordinary transformations with the creation of musicals. Nostradamus explains that musicals "appear to be a play where the dialogue stops, and the plot is conveyed through songs."[1] Among his predictions, he foresees that some musicals will be sung from beginning to end and explains how these musicals will work: "There's no talking and they often stay on one note for a very long time so that when they change to a different note, you notice. And it's supposed to create a dramatic effect. But mostly you just sit there asking yourself, 'why aren't they talking?'"[2] Laughter ensues as Nostradamus himself changes the note of the patter when he sings about the audience noticing the change.

In the American musical theater, the most typical form of structuring musicals has been the book musical, in which songs interrupt spoken dialogue and provide additional means to depict the characters and dramatic situations. The book musical started achieving supremacy in the 1940s, especially in the works of Rodgers and Hammerstein, Lerner and Loewe, and Kurt Weill. Other forms of musical theater were still popular in that decade, such as revues and operettas, but such emphasis on enhancing the book of musical comedies, as Kim Kowalke writes, "nurtured a new generation of talent who 'integrated' in their own versatile performances the particular combination of acting, dancing, and singing that made the American musical theater so distinctive from other forms of lyric drama."[3] Between the 1940s and the 1970s, creators of book musicals devised different ways to explore the partnership and tensions between narrative and musical performances, such as the musical play and the concept musical, while simultaneously renovating, or perhaps reinventing, musical comedy.[4] In any case,

---

[1] Wayne Kirkpatrick, Karey Kirkpatrick, John O'Farrell, Brian d'Arcy James, John Cariani, Heidi Blickenstaff, Brad Oscar, Kate Reinders, Brooks Ashmanskas, Peter Bartlett, and Christian Borle, *Something Rotten!: A Very New Musical; Original Broadway Cast Recording*, 1 audio disc (59:11): digital (New York: Ghostlight Records, 2015), 10.

[2] Kirkpatrick et al., *Something Rotten!* 10.

[3] Kim H. Kowalke, "Theorizing the Golden Age Musical: Genre, Structure, Syntax," in *A Music-Theoretical Matrix: Essays in Honor of Allen Forte (Part V)*, ed. David Carson Berry, *Gamut* 6, no. 2 (2013): 137.

[4] Larry Stempel explains how some musicals after 1940 can be categorized as musical plays (such as *Oklahoma!* and *My Fair Lady*), while others prolonged the life of musical comedy (such as *Finian's Rainbow* and *The Pajama Game*). Stempel also argues for the 1940s as a watershed decade in the development of the American musical (Larry Stempel, *Showtime: A History of the*

the book musical has always presented a conspicuous alternation of songs and spoken dialogue. As composer Jerry Herman once put it, "It is this rollercoaster between dialogue and song, this homogenization of the spoken and the sung word, that makes a career in the theater so fascinating."[5]

In the last quarter of the twentieth century, another form of structuring musicals – the one that is sung from beginning to end – came to prominence, especially with the arrival of several examples from London such as *Evita* (1979), *Cats* (1983), and *Miss Saigon* (1991).[6] Sung-through musicals distance themselves from the book musical by changing the balance between talking and singing, creating musicals in which the entire script – including monologues, conversations, turning points, and asides – is sung. This does not mean that sung-through musicals lack a book. They do feature a dramatic arc that shows how, where, and when a character goes from one situation to another. The difference lies in the structure of the book: instead of alternating between spoken dialogue and song, the book of a sung-through musical depends on a sequence of songs and continuous music that creates and develops dramatic action.

Starting in the 1970s and 1980s, the sung-through format started being used in musicals with a variety of techniques that challenged the conventions of the book musical. Creative teams (composers, lyricists, and book writers) employed specific procedures and compositional techniques through which music establishes characterization and expression when very little or nothing is spoken. Some sung-through musicals use songs alone to create and organize dramaturgy; others unevenly alternate between sung dialogue and a few spoken passages with underscoring, which erase the boundaries of dialogue and song and assign particular functions to the few spoken passages. These latter ones weave the music into the script in a way that, as critic Ben Brantley described in his review of *Fun Home*, "You'll find yourself hard pressed to recall what exactly was said and what was sung."[7] Scholarship on British sung-through musicals has demonstrated how some works fit the aesthetics of rock musicals (*Jesus Christ Superstar* [1971]), others the megamusical (*The Phantom of the Opera* [1986] and *Les*

Broadway Musical Theater [New York: W. W. Norton, 2010], 293–311 and 419–58). Kim Kowalke discusses the differences among "subtypes of the book musical" after 1940 (Kim H. Kowalke, "Theorizing the Golden Age Musical," 159–67). For a definition of the concept musical, see bruce mcclung, *Lady in the Dark: Biography of a Musical* (New York: Oxford University Press, 2007), 154–66.

[5] Jerry Herman, "The American Musical: Still Glowin', Stil Crowin', Still Goin' Strong," in *Playwrights, Lyricists, Composers on Theater*, ed. Otis L. Guernsey, Jr. (New York: Dodd, Mead & Co., 1974), 129.

[6] These years refer to these musicals' Broadway openings.

[7] Ben Brantley, "'Fun Home' at the Circle in the Square Theater," *New York Times*, April 19, 2015.

Misérables [1987]), while some others do not fit any particular subcategory (*Aspects of Love* [1990]), revealing this as a diverse group of musicals that were created using different compositional devices and dramaturgical structures.[8] Creators of musicals, audiences, and scholars like to create genres (or subgenres) based on common elements (e.g., musical comedy, revue, rock musical, jukebox musical) in an effort to discern a huge number of approaches that fall under the category "musical theatre." While the works we have placed in these categories share many features, they also differ from each other in significant ways. A Gershwin musical comedy differs from one by Cole Porter or Rodgers and Hart. This Element shows that this is also the case with the sung-through musical, a form of structuring music and lyrics to which different creators add variations and nuances that invite audiences to experience musical theater in innovative ways.

Such variety reveals that there is no single aesthetic for this form of musical theater but rather the sung-through musical embraces a range of structures that question the limits between singing and speaking. Not only did these structural alterations blur the differences between what is spoken and what is sung, but they also effaced the lines between song lyrics and the book of a musical, since these two can now be equaled. This Element is about American musicals that have little or no speech, and it explores some of the structures and processes through which they were created, thus demonstrating such variety within the sung-through musical. The selected musicals discussed here have been developed through devised or collaborative processes and small-scale early productions since the 1980s. Identifying their compositional methods and how the creators constructed the dramaturgy of their sung-through scores reveals how musical theater developed and reinvented itself toward and into the twenty-first century, challenging and repurposing some of its own conventions.

The methodology in this Element mirrors such diversity. Arguments, observations, and conclusions are drawn from musical and dramatic analyses of the selected musicals and information on the creative collaborative processes and reception. My research revealed manifold approaches to constructing and structuring sung-through musicals, and consequently, the varying levels of musicological and dramaturgical analysis in the sections are conspicuous. Some sections are more analytical with detailed information about the recurrence of musical themes, while others will focus more on creative process and collaboration. Such

---

[8] These years refer to these musicals' Broadway openings. For more on British sung-through musicals, see John Snelson, *Andrew Lloyd Webber* (New Haven: Yale University Press, 2004), Jessica Sternfeld, *The Megamusical* (Bloomington: Indiana University Press, 2006), and Bradley Rogers, *The Song Is You: Musical Theatre and the Politics of Bursting into Song and Dance* (Iowa City: University of Iowa Press, 2020), 180–99.

focus on analysis, process, or both offers different models for investigating this repertoire. As new musicals and approaches to the sung-through format are introduced, each section functions as a song in a song cycle, and when considered together, they expose the larger fabric in which they exist.[9]

Thus, each section explores a different dimension and particular elements of sung-through musicals from 1980 to the late 2010s. This Element is a study on aesthetics, not a historical survey of the sung-through musical, which explains why some works from that time period are not included. However, the musicals discussed here produce what Scott McMillin calls "a historical trajectory under-pinning the argument," a "historical silhouette"[10] that evinces the sung-through musical's place in late twentieth-century and early twenty-first-century musical theater, as they played on and off Broadway concurrently with many book musicals, including subcategories thereof, such as revivals and jukebox musicals.

More than an aesthetic change, the sung-through musical became emblematic and marked the musical theater experience of a generation. In a 2020 interview, Neil Patrick Harris was asked about the moment when he realized that he wanted to be an actor, singer, and dancer. He answered with the story of when he saw *Les Misérables* for the first time.[11] If Rodgers and Hammerstein, Lerner and Lowe, Jerome Robbins, Bob Fosse, Stephen Sondheim, and Michael Bennett introduced many young fans and performers to the world of musical theater in previous decades, sung-through musicals after 1980, such as *Les Misérables*, *Evita*, *Falsettos*, *Fun Home*, and *Hamilton*, to name a few, had an impact on the creation and formation of new musical theater audiences and performers. Sondheim confirmed this shift in a 2011 interview: "If you're talking about the musical in which there's speech and song, speech and song, it didn't die so much as become subsumed by the success of the sung-through musicals, mainly stemming from Britain. And audiences now are very used to the sung-through musical."[12]

Predecessors to the Sung-Through Structure

Some American musicals from before 1980 challenged the balance between singing and speaking established by the book musical and paved the way for the

---

[9] This Element does not consider revues from after 1980, which are sung-through plotless musicals whose songs either pertain to the same topic or are grouped in the same musical because they are by the same composer. Examples include *Marry Me a Little* (1981), *Songs for a New World* (1995), *Smokey Joe's Café* (1995), and *Bring in 'da Noise, Bring in 'da Funk* (1995). It also does not consider sung-through musicals composed for regional theaters throughout the United States or those composed in New York City's Off-Off-Broadway circuit, such as *Charlotte Sweet* (1982).

[10] Scott McMillin, *The Musical as Drama* (Princeton: Princeton University Press, 2006), xi.

[11] Michael Paulson, "Offstage: How I Miss Broadway," live stream, *New York Times*, October 1, 2020.

[12] Quoted in Richard Eyre, "Talking Theatre with Stephen Sondheim," *Play Ground*, July 22, 2011, https://nickhernbooksblog.com/2011/07/22/talkingtheatre_stephensondheim.

works considered here. Predecessors in this respect include the three satirical operettas by George and Ira Gershwin from the early 1930s: *Strike Up the Band* (1927; 1930 Broadway), *Of Thee I Sing* (1931), and *Let 'em Eat Cake* (1933). These three works helped innovate musical theater by combining typical musical numbers of operetta (such as the sung-through finaletto) with elements of musical comedy. Ira explained that in *Of Thee I Sing*:

> There are no verse-and-chorus songs; there is a sort of recitative running along, and lots of finales and finalettos. . . . It is hard to sit down and stretch out some single song for thirty-two measures. That is what you do with the usual song. In this show you develop ideas, condensing pages of possible dialogue into a few lines of song.[13]

Operettas of the 1910s and 1920s alternated between spoken dialogue and musical numbers and included extended sung-through finales. American operettas on Broadway and the dramaturgical and musical structures of their sung-through finales paved the way for much of the developments in musical theater in the 1940s.[14] In addition, Larry Stempel has shown that in the middle decades of the twentieth century, Broadway saw works that merged operatic forms and conventions with "adopt[ed] vernacular musical idioms and closed musical forms [and] the use of spoken dialogue at times."[15] Among these "Broadway Operas," he discusses the form and content of the Gershwin brothers and DuBose Heyward's *Porgy and Bess* (1935) and Kurt Weill's *Street Scene* (1947). Weill himself defended and wrote about the practice of combining operatic traditions with the Broadway musical.[16]

In the early 1950s, while musicals like *Guys and Dolls*, *The King and I*, and *Wonderful Town* were proving (or at least testing) the legacy of how "integrated" the elements of musical theater could be, Jerome Moross and John Latouche's *The Golden Apple* (1954) revealed a new and unique form of integration. This musical dramatized an American adaptation of Homer's epic poems the *Iliad* and the *Odyssey* with only songs and no spoken dialogue. As critic Richard Watts Jr. astutely noted, "It is a play in music, rather than a play with music."[17] Moross came up with the idea of making the musical entirely sung. He stated, "Our approach to the lyrical theatre was to use the best in musical comedy, opera, and ballet forms with gay abandon, and we were

---

[13] Quoted in Philip Furia, *Ira Gershwin: The Art of the Lyricist* (New York: Oxford University Press, 1996), 91.

[14] William A. Everett, "Golden Days in Old Heidelberg: The First-Act Finale of Sigmund Romberg's *The Student Prince*," *American Music* 12, no. 3 (1994): 255–82.

[15] Stempel, *Showtime*, 371.

[16] Stephen Hinton, *Weill's Musical Theater: Stages of Reform* (Berkeley: University of California Press, 2012). For more on Broadway Opera, see Stempel, *Showtime*, 369–97.

[17] Richard Watts, Jr., "Review of *The Golden Apple*," *New York Post*, March 12, 1954.

convinced that the resulting mixture would allow us both to entertain and say what we had to say."[18] Latouche went further, arguing that:

> The result is completely different from such forms as opera and ballet. It develops out of musical comedy, consisting of what can be called a series of interlocking production numbers. The sung dialogue, instead of the artificial recitative of opera, is rendered in short songs whose separate melodies become part of the major production number.... The absence of a spoken text allows ... moments to find their proper adjustments, even allows breaking all the rules when necessary, to achieve a definite result.[19]

Moross and Latouche's ambitious work can thus be considered as the main precursor of the sung-through format.

Another sung-through musical that deserves attention is *The Umbrellas of Cherbourg*, an adaptation of the 1964 French-German film in which composer Michel Legrand set every line of dialogue to music. Director Andrei Serban and lyricist Sheldon Harnick created the stage version, which played Off-Broadway from February 1 to March 4, 1979. The production found favor with critics and audiences, and rumor had it throughout the rest of the 1978–1979 season that it would move to Broadway, but it never did.[20] Although this sung-through musical never entered the standard American musical repertoire, it has found audiences in regional theaters in the United States as well as in London.

These works not only challenged the supremacy of the book musical but also proved that reshaping of the musical theatre form could succeed as popular entertainment. The post-1980 American musicals considered in this Element continued and expanded these works' innovations and demonstrate that dissolving the differences between singing and speaking, and book and lyrics, has become an important element of musical theater.

2 Opera or Broadway Musical: *The Human Comedy*

On October 20, 1983, a memo from The New York Shakespeare Festival Public Theater to its department heads invited them "to an open reading of *The Human Comedy*, an opera-musical composed by Galt MacDermot [1928–2018], with a libretto by William Dumaresq [1930–1998] based on William Saroyan's novel," that took place the following day.[21] Perhaps more noticeable than the

---

[18] Jerome Moross and John Latouche, *The Golden Apple: A Musical in Two Acts* (New York: Random House, 1954), xix.

[19] Moross and Latouche, *The Golden Apple*, xv–xvi and xiii.

[20] Dan Dietz, *Off-Broadway Musicals, 1910–2007: Casts, Credits, Songs, Critical Reception and Performance Data of More than 1800 Shows* (Jefferson, NC: McFarland, 2010), 471.

[21] Memo from Gail Merrifield to Department Heads, The New York Shakespeare Festival Records, New York Public Library for the Performing Arts, Billy Rose Theatre Division.

fact that this was a new work by the composer of the legendary musical *Hair* is the moniker used to describe it: opera-musical. Uncertain what to call or which genre to label this sung-through musical, the author of the memo decided on an agglutination of terms that does not exactly inform the reader what the work is. As *The Human Comedy* developed and premiered at The Public Theater and eventually moved to Broadway, journalists and critics used several other terms to refer to it, including musical, folk opera, pop opera, pop-folk opera, cantata, pop cantata, and oratorio.

Based on Saroyan's 1943 eponymous film and subsequent novel, *The Human Comedy* is the story of Homer Macaulay, a young boy who works as a telegram messenger in the fictitious town of Ithaca, California, in the early days of World War II. He lives with his widowed mother and two siblings, his sister Bess and his brother Ulysses, the youngest of the Macaulays. Homer's older brother, Marcus, is fighting in Europe. Homer starts working at Spangler's telegraph office after school to help his mother with the family income. Spangler and Mr. Grogan (an elderly alcoholic man) receive the telegraphs, and Homer delivers them to their recipients all over town. The messages bring images and impacts of the war to the small town and affect its everyday activities. The job helps Homer mature and understand the hardships of life. His little brother, Ulysses, too young to understand the war, innocently explores his hometown and is always asking questions about the meaning of everything around him.

The Human Comedy straddles the boundary between opera and the Broadway musical. MacDermot himself referred to the work as an opera, and for that reason, it had to be sung from beginning to end.[22] The composer's preferred label stems from the fact that the project started as an opera commission from the Banff Centre for Arts and Creativity in Banff, Alberta, Canada. (MacDermot was born in Canada.) He spent three years deciding on a story and first came across Saroyan's novel in Christmas 1981 when his brother-in-law had each of the family's children read an excerpt from a literary work, and MacDermot's son was assigned an excerpt from *The Human Comedy*. MacDermot read the novel afterward and settled on its story for his opera.[23]

MacDermot believed that not only was the sung-through format appropriate for an opera, but it was also the best musical means to advance the suspension of disbelief that infuses Saroyan's narrative. MacDermot explained:

> In most plays, people talk like they talk, but in this one they don't say normal things. [In the scene] [w]hen the thief comes in and the guy [Spangler] tells

[22] Galt MacDermot, interview by author, New York, June 16, 2015.
[23] Leslie Bennetts, "Holiday Party Inspired 'Human Comedy' Opera," *New York Times*, January 2, 1984.

him to take the money, the guy is almost happy about it. The things people say to each other in *The Human Comedy* are totally unlike things people say; they're in another realm. I think that's good for a musical, because music isn't a real thing, people don't really sing to each other. So when you're singing, other rules of behavior and common-sense reality are suspended. I found that Saroyan had suspended it already in the novel.[24]

In his review of the Off-Broadway production, Frank Rich observed that Saroyan's book introduced a suspension of reality also by being set in a fictional town "where even the poor give to charity, where thieves are disarmed by kindness, and where ethnic and racial differences are a cause for celebration."[25] It seems that Saroyan's plot and characters naturally lent themselves to a sung-through score in which lines like "how do you do?" and "I like nothing better than coconut cream pie" can be sung without disrupting theatrical illusion. To support the suspension of disbelief, the original production had nominal scenery (some chairs and a few props) and minimal period costumes, and both the cast and the orchestra remained present on stage the entire time, watching the action when not part of it.

Shortly after receiving the commission from the Banff Centre, MacDermot invited Dumaresq to write the book and lyrics for *The Human Comedy*. They had worked together on previous projects, including a 1970 London musical titled *Isabel's a Jezebel* and the 1975 contemporary mass setting, *Take This Bread: 'A Mass in Our Time'*. They had also performed as the folk duo Angus and Fergus MacRoy.[26] Dumaresq penned the script first, and probably because of the prospect of an opera, he metered every line of dialogue, which feature internal and end rhymes. MacDermot musicalized the entire script in two months and later orchestrated it for the original production.[27] He segmented his opera into songs, recitatives, and interludes that flow uninterruptedly and acquire the operatic functions of arias, ariosos, duets, trios, and choral numbers. Dumaresq wrote what was going to be sung dialogue, monologue, ensembles, or comment on the action by the chorus, but MacDermot took the liberty of adapting the choral passages for soloists and vice versa. In several instances the chorus provides musical accompaniment to the soloists. MacDermot made many of these changes during the workshops that took place at The Public Theater in 1983, for when he realized that he was working with very fine singers, he knew he would be able to create variety through his handling of the voices.[28]

---

[24] Bennetts, "Holiday Party Inspired 'Human Comedy' Opera."

[25] Frank Rich, "Saroyan Set to Music," *New York Times*, December 29, 1983.

[26] MacDermot, interview by author, June 16, 2015.

[27] MacDermot, interview by author, June 16, 2015.

[28] MacDermot, interview by author, June 16, 2015.

After MacDermot and Dumaresq had started working on *The Human Comedy*, the Canadian commissioner expressed disapproval over funding an opera based on an American novel and requested that they change the locale from California to Canada. MacDermot refused, canceled the commission, and invited Dumaresq to look for potential producers in the United States.[29] In spring 1983, after some unsuccessful auditions, MacDermot reached out to producer Joseph Papp (1921–1991) of The Public Theater, who had already produced MacDermot's two most successful musicals, *Hair* (1967) and *The Two Gentlemen of Verona* (1971). The Public Theater had recently begun presenting opera with its 1980 production of Gilbert and Sullivan's *The Pirates of Penzance* at Central Park's Delacorte Theater, which later transferred to Broadway (when it won the Tony Award for best revival in 1981) and became the basis for the 1983 film version. Papp was impressed with what he saw of MacDermot and Dumaresq's opera and brought two names from the production of *Penzance* to develop it: director Wilford Leach and actor Rex Smith, who played Frederic in *Penzance* (in both the stage and film versions) and would create the role of Spangler in *The Human Comedy*.

MacDermot believed that Papp was the only producer in New York at that time who would agree to produce a piece of theater that was entirely sung.[30] He stated, "Joe Papp . . . was very open to everything . . . He loved that show, the story . . . and only Joe Papp would do such a thing."[31] Papp himself became involved with the production, not only because of its unconventional structure but also because it tapped into memories of his own childhood and young adulthood. The producer went on to make several radio and television commercials for *The Human Comedy*, and his photograph was featured on posters for the production throughout the city as well as the playbill.[32] *The Human Comedy* had a mildly successful run of seventy-nine performances at The Public Theater (from December 28, 1983, to March 4, 1984). Positive reviews prompted Papp to take it to Broadway in a partnership with the Shubert Organization. *The Human Comedy* opened at the Royale Theatre (the Bernard B. Jacobs Theatre in 2022) on April 5, 1984, where it ran for nineteen previews and only thirteen performances, closing on April 15. During its stay at the Royale, Papp's face moved beyond printed materials to also appear on the theater's marquee.[33]

---

[29] Galt MacDermot, interview by Kenneth Turan, March 26, 1987, Joseph Papp Oral History Interviews, New York Public Library for the Performing Arts, New York.

[30] MacDermot, interview by author, June 16, 2015.

[31] MacDermot, interview by author, June 16, 2015.

[32] Samuel G. Freedman, "'Human Comedy' Moves to Broadway," *New York Times*, April 5, 1984.

[33] Freedman, "'Human Comedy' Moves to Broadway." Among the reasons why the show flopped on Broadway was that very little was changed in Leach's staging when *The Human Comedy* moved to Broadway, and the small setting that worked well at the Anspacher Theater (at the

Neither sketches of Dumaresq's script nor MacDermot's score[34] include a segmentation of *The Human Comedy* into songs. Rather, they indicate that both creators saw the work as continuous dramatic action with continuous music. The program for the Off-Broadway run did not include any song titles, just the locales in which each scene takes place ("at home," "at school," "telegraph office," "train crossing," "war front," etc.).[35] The playbill for the Broadway production, however, listed some, though not all, song titles, suggesting that the production team may have been concerned about how audiences would react to its operatic continuity. The dramatic action includes the same locales as in the Off-Broadway playbill along with forty-five songs: twenty-four in the first act and twenty-one in the second.[36] Short passages, such as sung dialogues ("Mama," "What Do I Sing?" and "Come On, Toby") and those in which the chorus narrates or comments on the action ("Mary Arena," "As the Poet Said," and "Slowly the Reality"), do not appear in the playbill.[37] Thus, the songs that do appear become units of the dramatic action that communicate to the audience changes in character and scenery configurations, as a song list traditionally does in a book musical.[38]

Throughout the centuries, operas have employed multiple musical styles in their scores. MacDermot followed suit with a score that relies on various genres and styles of popular music and which strengthens connections to music from outside the theater. Jazz musicians (especially Duke Ellington) fascinated MacDermot from an early age and inspired him to follow a career in music. He studied composition in Cape Town, South Africa, where he was exposed to many musical genres, and he later worked as a church organist in

Public, with 275 seats) felt out of place in a Broadway house with 1,078 seats. It also faced fierce competition in the 1983–1984 season, including *La Cage aux Folles*, *Sunday in the Park with George*, *Baby*, *The Tap Dance Kid*, and *The Rink*.

[34] Both are extant in the Joseph Papp papers at the New York Public Library for the Performing Arts.

[35] Showbill, New York Shakespeare Festival Public Theater, Anspacher Theater, *The Human Comedy* (January 1984): 17.

[36] *The Human Comedy*, Royale Theatre, *Playbill*, 2, no. 6 (March 1984): 41–42.

[37] This same division of the action into locales and forty-five songs appears in the first pages of the published libretto. William Dumaresq and Galt MacDermot, *The Human Comedy* (New York: Samuel French, 1985), 8–9.

[38] The original cast recording contains the entire show and breaks MacDermot's score into eighty-six songs, whose titles are all provided. The original cast recorded the musical in 1984, and a US $138,000 donation by Ivan Boesky – as a former trustee of the New York Shakespeare Festival – funded the album (a letter from Papp to the Southern District Court of New York, dated October 6, 1987, confirming the donation and the use of the money, survives in the New York Shakespeare Festival Records, New York Public Library for the Performing Arts, Billy Rose Theatre Division). It is not entirely clear why, but the recording was not made commercially available after the Broadway run, although the fact that the musical flopped on Broadway may explain Papp's decision. The album was released as a two-CD set in 1997 by Kilmarnock Records.

his hometown of Montréal. By the time he arrived in New York City in 1964, he had also become a fan of rock music and wanted to use all these musical styles in his compositions. When he learned about the content of *Hair*, MacDermot realized that mixing all the musical styles with which he was familiar was going to enhance the musical's agenda. He explained: "[James Rado and Gerome Ragni, the creators of *Hair*] did not want the show to throw back to the old idiom of Broadway musicals. I didn't really like that style of music, so I was fine with getting rid of that sound altogether."[39] *Hair*'s music ranges from ballads to psychedelic rock, funk, country, and soul. The score offers a pastiche of musical styles that confronted musical theater songwriting in 1967 in the same way that the show's sardonic attitudes criticized American values and the Vietnam War.

When he composed the music for *The Human Comedy*, MacDermot exercised the same method of employing musical variety, except now in a sung-through format. He created a musical architecture that blends many different musical styles and genres and attributes them to specific characters and situations. For example, the curious Ulysses asks his mother about the world around him using country music ("Mama"); the Macaulay family sings about their situation in slow ballads whose accompaniments and countermelodies, played by a guitar and violins, provide a folk flavor to the score ("We're a Little Family," "The Birds in the Sky," "Remember Always to Give," "The World Is Full of Loneliness," and "Dear Brother Homer"); and the chorus intervenes and comments on the action in gospel songs ("Beautiful Music," "Long Past Sunset," "As the Poet Said," and "Fathers and Mothers"). Many of the characters use jitterbug and swing music to express cheerfulness, such as Homer in "Noses," Bess and Mary in "I Let Him Kiss Me Once," Marcus in "My Sister Bess," Diana in "I've Known a Lot of Guys," and Spangler in "Diana." The boys on the war front sing barbershop ballads, such as "How I Love" and "Everlasting." The interludes, "Bicycle Ride," "Train," and "Nightmare," reveal MacDermot's jazz influences, even with calls for improvisation (at least in his original orchestration) in the piano and saxophone parts.

MacDermot also composed songs that feature elements of 1970s pop music (a steady drumbeat, a strumming guitar providing harmony, and a bass, all accompanying diatonic melodies). In addition to wide vocal ranges and uses of parlando, these pop-flavored songs become powerful monologues for the main characters ("Everything Is Changed," "I Don't Know Who to Hate," and "I'll Always Love You"). Clive Barnes's description of MacDermot's score for *Hair* seems apropos for *The Human Comedy*: it "appeal[s] to people who like *The*

---

[39] MacDermot, interview by Kenneth Turan, March 26, 1987.

Sound of Music as well as the sound of music."[40] Such variety in a single sung-through score blurs the lines between genres, making terms like musical, pop opera, and pop-folk opera all perfectly applicable.

Musical variety in *The Human Comedy* mirrors and emphasizes the inherent diversity of Dumaresq's script, which in turn follows Saroyan's film and novel. The musical presents a plethora of contrasting topics ranging from celebrating life to coping with death. A couple that has recently fallen in love (Spangler and Diana) contrasts with the tale of a widow who is bearing the loss of her husband and son (Homer's mother, Kate). Characters of various ages face hard situations, from young Ulysses and his curiosity about the world around him and Homer realizing that the war in Europe has ramifications in his Californian hometown to Mr. Grogan, the oldest of all characters, whose heart cannot take it when he has to tell his young co-worker that his brother died in action.

Critics noticed how crucial such musical variety was to the story. Clive Barnes wrote that MacDermot's music "runs the narrow line between creativity and pastiche, and it not only evokes its own period but also contrives to maintain its own contemporary validity."[41] Michael Feingold argued that the "music has the power to transcend the dubious parts of [Saroyan's novel] and intensify the good ones," and MacDermot accomplished this by using "a rhythm, usually in some familiar dance form, to define each short scene; dances that reflect the period of the work [1940s], like the rhumba and the jitterbug, are jostled by gavotte and tarantella on one side, waltz clog and the strict 4/4 of English folk ballads on the other."[42] Frank Rich noted that the musical complements Saroyan's novel, pointing out that "as befits Saroyan's pantheistic sense of community, the music is also highly eclectic: it encompasses gospel, jazz, swing, hymns, barbershop harmonies, blues, and plaintive lullabies that almost might have been written by Woody Guthrie." Rich also argued that *The Human Comedy* was "a lovely show that is far closer to *Hair* than one might expect," claiming that both musicals "subscribe to the same fairy-tale dream of democracy: wars come and go, but justice is their only ideological creed."[43] Barnes also drew comparisons with *Hair*, including MacDermot's music and the musicals' unusual structures: "Both are concerned with wars ... with soldiers going off to fight, and the people they leave behind, both look at death, both incorporate appropriate music into their fabric ... neither musical has a formal book .... In both the story is told almost by inference, as the characters emerge

---

[40] Clive Barnes, *"Hair* Is a Shaggy Happening Set to Rock Music that Grooves Along with Pot, Peaceniks and a Startling Tableau of Nudes," *Saturday Evening Post*, August 10, 1968.

[41] Clive Barnes, "'Human Comedy': All Sugar, No Spice," *New York Post*, December 29, 1983.

[42] Michael Feingold, "Sentimental Block," *Village Voice*, January 10, 1984.

[43] Rich, "Saroyan Set to Music."

from their backgrounds."[44] *Hair* and *The Human Comedy* both make strong social commentaries, messages that are enhanced through MacDermot's musical eclecticism.

In the case of *The Human Comedy*, compositional technique transcends the labeling of the work as opera or musical, since both traditions have relied on musical pastiche to dramatize stories on stage. MacDermot confirmed that he employed musical variety because it is an effective method: "Music is a very tricky thing. It can get boring. So you got to change it. And that means changing the style, changing all the ingredients . . . and that's really the basis of working in the theater: it's variety."[45]

The Human Comedy in Context

MacDermot composed two sung-through scores before *The Human Comedy*, both for Broadway. Both flopped. *Dude* opened on October 9, 1972, and reunited MacDermot with lyricist and book writer Gerome Ragni and director Tom O'Horgan, with whom he had worked on *Hair*. The musical's title refers to the main character, an unnamed everyman who is tempted by the forces of good and evil. Ken Mandelbaum has claimed that this was "perhaps the most incomprehensible show ever presented on a Broadway stage, it was mostly sung, but its songs were barely related and could have been performed in any order or by any 'character' with the same result."[46] *Dude* played sixteen performances before closing. *Via Galactica* opened on November 28, 1972, and was created by director Peter Hall. Christopher Gore penned the book and lyrics. MacDermot and Gore's songs portrayed life on an asteroid in the year 2972. MacDermot was unlucky for the second time in the same season to provide the music for a confusing book, which critics panned, and this production closed after just eight performances. *The Human Comedy* holds a unique place in McDermmot's musical theater output. It was not a hit like *Hair* and *Two Gentlemen of Verona*, but because of its successful Off-Broadway run and afterlife in regional theaters and colleges, it was not the fiasco of *Dude* and *Via Galactica*.

The Human Comedy is a hybrid of success and failure, opera and musical theater, reigniting similar discussions concerning *The Golden Apple*, which in turn have their own connections with mid-century Broadway opera.[47] Therefore, *The Human Comedy* extended the debate over genre confusion, something that composer Michael John LaChiusa defines as a "cross-pollination of genres . . . the only way for music theater to thrive [because] [i]f there is an American aesthetic,

---

[44] Barnes, "'Human Comedy'."   [45] MacDermot, interview by author, June 16, 2015.

[46] Ken Mandelbaum, *Not since Carrie: Forty Years of Broadway Musical Flops* (New York: St. Martin's Press, 1992), 23.

[47] See the Introduction to this Element.

it's all-embracing."[48] MacDermot and Dumaresq's *The Human Comedy* did not introduce sung-through as something new, but it reactivated a form that the American musical theater had employed earlier, reinforcing the confluence of musical and theatrical genres that defines the American musical.

3 "You Hear It Sung . . . and the World Seems Different": William Finn's Sung-Through Scores

In the late 1970s, when William Finn (b. 1952) moved to New York City, he often invited his friends Mary Testa, Alison Fraser, and Kay Passick to come to his apartment, cook together, and sing some of his new songs. As he tailored music and lyrics to the four performers, the character of Marvin gradually emerged, accompanied by songs that addressed Marvin's adolescence and sexuality. This is how the Marvin musicals, which would form a trilogy of Off-Broadway musicals in the 1980s, two of which would become the Broadway musical *Falsettos* in the early 1990s, were born. Finn has admitted that he is not a playwright and lacks the skills to structure a plot, so writing songs was always the best way to develop character or fill in dramatic gaps. He claimed, "I didn't know how to write a book, that's why I wrote all sung. It's not like I wanted to write all sung."[49]

Finn's approach to the sung-through musical came about almost accidentally and owes a great deal to director James Lapine (b. 1949). In addition to their extraordinary mode of musical-dramatic presentation, Finn's sung-through scores tell the stories of exceptional characters, gay men, and the people who love them, in ways that defy media stereotypes of the time. In these works, innovations in form and content support and complement one another.

Between 1978 and 1998, Finn created four one-act sung-through musicals for which he wrote both music and lyrics: the Marvin musicals – *In Trousers* (1979, revised in 1981 and 1985), *March of the Falsettos* (1981), and *Falsettoland* (1990) – and *A New Brain* (1998). *March of the Falsettos* and *Falsettoland* became the two acts of *Falsettos* (1992). What makes Finn's sung-through scores unique is that he does not resort to either spoken or sung dialogue (or recitative) between songs, which means that these musicals' books are entirely composed of song lyrics. The structure resembles that of a song cycle, as the dramatic action moves from one self-contained song to another. The genesis and early performance histories of these musicals show how a string of songs can be morphed into highly effective storytelling.

---

[48]　Michael John LaChiusa, "Genre Confusion," *Opera News* 67, no. 2 (August 2002): 73.

[49]　William Finn, interview by author, New York, May 21, 2013.

In Trousers

The first musical in the Marvin trilogy focuses on how Marvin struggles to understand and accept his sexuality. Its story alternates between the present (when Marvin is married, has a son, and realizes he prefers to be with men) and the past (when he recalls his high school sweetheart, his high school English teacher – Miss Goldberg – and also his first sexual experience with another man, Whizzer). While revisiting his teenage years, Marvin remembers the story of Christopher Columbus and Amerigo Vespucci's arrival in America. In Marvin's imagination, Columbus named the New World America because he had an affair with Vespucci. Marvin, thus, realizes that desire for men has always been part of his sexual identity and finally decides that he will enter into relationships with men.

The title of the musical refers to gender identification. As Marvin explores his past and his present, he begins to accept that he is interested in people in trousers (men) more than people in dresses (women). The three ladies (Marvin's wife, his high school sweetheart, and Miss Goldberg) begin the musical dressed in trousers, and as they perform the first song, to quote the script, they "reveal their dresses underneath" and "play the remainder of the show in these dresses."[50] Clothing was so crucial in enhancing the gender issues in the musical that the original production listed the characters based on what they wore and not by their names: with the pink shirt (the wife), with the blond hair (the high school sweetheart), with the sunglasses (Miss Goldberg), and with the sneakers (Marvin).[51]

In Trousers was not conceived with an eventual trilogy in mind. It developed from those gatherings with Testa, Fraser, and Passick, who originated the roles of Miss Goldberg, the wife, and the sweetheart, respectively. Their input and talent prompted Finn to compose additional songs about Marvin and the women in his life. As Finn explains, the musical slowly became

> a bunch of cabaret songs called *In Trousers* and that was for three women and a man. And it was about a petulant guy named Marvin. Whenever things got too hot for him, he'd revert back to himself when he was fourteen, just kind of childish, hysterical guy. He was leaving his wife for a man. He was having these fantasies about men. He didn't know how to deal with them. ... So whenever things would get hot for him, he would leave. That developed into the first of these Marvin shows.[52]

---

[50] William Finn, *In Trousers* (New York: Samuel French, 1986), 10.

[51] Richard Eder, "'In Trousers' Is Fantasies of a Boy, 14," *New York Times*, March 17, 1979.

[52] William Finn, interview by Ruth Simon, June 6, 1993, in the New York Public Library for the Performing Arts Digital Collections, http://digitalcollections.nypl.org/items/4f9bf9c0-02e9-0131-a322-58d385a7b928#.

The early performances of *In Trousers* took place in Finn's living room, for which he borrowed chairs from the Jewish temple on 100th Street to accommodate his audience.[53] He played the piano and sang Marvin's part. The Off-Broadway theater Playwrights Horizons was in the process of founding a musical theater lab that, similar to what it had previously done with spoken drama, would offer the opportunity for composers, lyricists, and book writers to develop, workshop, and eventually stage their musicals. André Bishop, then Playwrights Horizons's artistic director, attended one of the performances in Finn's apartment and encouraged then the company's musical theater director, Ira Weitzman, to attend another. Weitzman did and subsequently offered to workshop *In Trousers* in the new musical theater lab.[54] Kay Passick left the project when it moved to Playwrights Horizons and was replaced by Joanna Green. Finn directed the production, and Chip Zien was cast to play the protagonist. This production was workshopped for eight performances beginning on December 8, 1978. It opened at Playwrights Horizons on February 21, 1979, and ran until March 18.

Unlike the next two Marvin musicals, the original production of *In Trousers* had no outside stage director to question or comment on Finn's choices in how he structured the musical. Finn admitted: "I didn't know that that would appeal to anyone. I thought that these were just quirky little songs that my friends and I would enjoy and that would be it. But things obviously take on a life of their own."[55] Although critics embraced Finn's songs and his musical style, they panned the musical's structure. Michael Feingold wrote, "The piece ... has virtually no script, and Finn's lyrics either wander elliptically all over the verbal map, or repeat themselves till they make Gertrude Stein look like a model of concision."[56] *The New York Times* critic described the musical as "eighteen songs and a few barely suggested sketches setting out the fantasies and worries of a fourteen-year-old boy named Marvin."[57] *In Trousers* was revived Off-Broadway and considerably rewritten twice during the 1980s, at Second Stage Theatre in 1981 and at the Promenade Theatre in 1985.[58] In both rewritings, Finn cut, added, and reordered songs but maintained the song-cycle structure.

Ironically, in all three versions, the plot's climax – when Marvin realizes and accepts his sexuality – does not occur in song. The number "How America Got Its Name" features a spoken play-within-a-musical in which the sweetheart

---

[53] Finn, interview by author, May 21, 2013.

[54] For an account of these events from Ira Weitzman's perspective, see Barry Singer, *Ever after: The Last Years of Musical Theater and Beyond* (New York: Applause, 2004), 11–17.

[55] Finn, interview by Ruth Simon, June 6, 1993.

[56] Michael Feingold, "Short Takes," *Village Voice*, March 12, 1979.

[57] Eder, "'In Trousers' Is Fantasies of a Boy, 14."

[58] Finn considers the 1985 version to be definitive, and it is now available for rental.

narrates Columbus's saga and supposed affair with Vespucci. Miss Goldberg plays Queen Isabella, and Marvin plays Columbus. This insertion does not disrupt the overall song-cycle structure of the musical since "How America Got Its Name" is bookended by music. At the end of the scene, the women reprise Miss Goldberg's song "Set Those Sails," and Marvin speaks the telling line, "The thing about explorers is: they discover things that are already there."[59] Finn chose not to musicalize most of this scene because he thought it would be a necessary break for the audience from all the singing.[60] In addition, this spoken passage predates the songs in Finn's compositional process. In one of the published versions of the lyrics for *In Trousers*, he confirms, "'How America Got Its Name' was written in 1978, at least two years before anyone had heard of a gay plague. What I was thinking when I wrote it, I have no idea."[61]

March of the Falsettos

Shortly after *In Trousers* closed, director James Lapine started workshopping his new play, *Table Settings*, at Playwrights Horizons. Finn watched it and loved the direction: "It was directed like a musical, and I felt it was really beautiful. And [André Bishop] said, 'Well, that's who I want you to work with'. He got us together."[62] Finn and Lapine teamed up to create a sequel to *In Trousers*. They maintained Marvin as the protagonist and also decided that Whizzer and Marvin's son (now named Jason) were going to appear on stage. They also named Marvin's wife Trina and decided to cut the characters of Marvin's high school sweetheart and Miss Goldberg.

Although openly gay in this sequel, Marvin still struggles with self-acceptance, which complicates his relationship with both Trina and Whizzer and makes him feel disconnected from Jason. Marvin's patriarchal values irritate Whizzer, who eventually leaves him. Marvin gets even more frustrated when Trina marries his psychiatrist, Mendel. At the end of *March of the Falsettos*, Marvin's relationships with both Whizzer and Trina are shattered. However, he makes amends with Jason, explaining that understanding and accepting one's sexuality is something that every man has to go through, and Jason will also have to do this as he grows up. The musical, thus, explores how men (and boys) struggle to find their voices in a society in which the definition of masculinity is rarely questioned.

---

[59] Finn, *In Trousers*, 77.   [60] William Finn, telephone interview with author, October 22, 2015.

[61] William Finn, *Falsettos: March of the Falsettos and Falsettoland by William Finn and James Lapine, and In Trousers by William Finn* (New York: Plume Drama, 1992), 226.

[62] Finn, interview by author, May 21, 2013.

Similar to *In Trousers*, Finn conceived *March of the Falsettos* as songs. The first number that he wrote was "Four Jews in a Room Bitching," which became the musical's working title and opening number. When Lapine reacted to it, Finn renamed the musical "The Pettiness of Misogyny," which emphasized Marvin's relationship with Trina. After Finn composed a second song for the show, "March of the Falsettos," the composer and director settled on this title for the musical and expanded the idea of the falsetto range in the male voice as a metaphor for masculinity. Finn explained: "Falsetto is a voice normally outside the normal range ... I felt these were people [the characters] whose situation was outside the normal range of most people's situation, and so I thought that falsettos kind of, in a vocal way, explained that."[63]

According to Finn, "Almost the whole show was written during the rehearsals" because "Lapine suggested things, and they would change everything, and so I would have to rewrite everything."[64] Actor Stephen Bogardus (who originated the role of Whizzer) claimed that "about a quarter of the material came in in the last ten days before our first public performance."[65] Lapine gathered the few songs that Finn had composed, wrote their titles on index cards, and organized them into a plot. Finn added:

> I'm not good at structure, and we have to face up to our strengths and weaknesses, and I was lucky that when I had to face up to my structural deficiencies, Lapine was right there to supplement all of it. . . . I get stuck, and when I get stuck, I get stuck, I don't write for three days . . . and Lapine gets you unstuck, he has the most fertile mind of anyone I've ever met. And he says, "Well, if that doesn't work, what about this, what about this?" It's all coming from a very clear place. . . . Lapine is very clear-headed.[66]

Lapine's participation in the creative process of *March of the Falsettos* produced a more cohesive musical than *In Trousers*. Finn concludes: "I find writing the songs very simple. What I find harder is deciding what the song is going to be about. So when you're working with Lapine, he can help you decide what the song is going to be about, and then I can write the songs easily."[67] The original production featured nineteen continuous songs that told the story of Marvin's struggles to come to terms with his ex-wife, son, and new male lover.

March of the Falsettos opened on May 20, 1981, at Playwrights Horizons, where it ran until September 26. It transferred to another Off-Broadway theater, the Westside Theater, wherein played 268 performances between October 13, 1981, and January 31, 1982. One critic's reaction to this musical reveals how

---

[63] Finn, interview by Ruth Simon, June 6, 1993.   [64] Finn, interview by author, May 21, 2013.

[65] Quoted in Marty Bell, *Broadway Stories: A Backstage Journey through Musical Theatre* (New York: Limelight, 1993), 22.

[66] Finn, interview by author, May 21, 2013.   [67] Finn, interview by Ruth Simon, June 6, 1993.

Finn's second musical and first commercial success challenged conventions of the American musical theater:

> We seem not to have words in our current vocabulary to easily label [Finn's musical]. Both [*March of the*] *Falsettos* and *In Trousers*, [Finn's] first work, are a collection of continuously performed songs with no dialogue between. To call it operetta suggests a formalism and stodginess that would rob Finn's work of its vitality, and to say it's a rock opera is too limiting of his musical diversity. Finn has created a popular, accessible, and classy contemporary musical idiom as the framework for his story.[68]

Falsettoland

Finn returned to Playwrights Horizons in the late 1980s, as the theater had agreed to produce a third musical for Marvin with the working title *Jason's Bar Mitzvah*. Finn and Lapine thought that Marvin's story needed closure, and the original idea was to set it around the preparation for Jason's bar mitzvah. However, by the end of the decade, they also thought that the AIDS pandemic's impact on the gay community could not be ignored and wanted to create a musical that portrayed daily life in the early days of the AIDS crisis. The plot thus alternates between the preparations for the bar mitzvah and Whizzer's succumbing to AIDS. Script readings for the new musical began in 1988, and in the following year, a workshop called *Marvin's Songs* presented *March of the Falsettos* in conjunction with some songs for the new musical.[69] Retitled *Falsettoland*, the third musical in the Marvin trilogy, opened at Playwrights Horizons on June 28, 1990, and closed on August 2. Its success prompted a transfer to another Off-Broadway theater, the Lucille Lortel Theater, where it opened on September 25, 1990, and ran for 176 performances, closing on January 27, 1991.

Finn and Lapine created the one-act *Falsettoland* with the intention of pairing it with *March of the Falsettos* as a double bill, necessitating another sung-through structure. Familiar with Finn's challenges in this regard, Lapine continued the creative process that they had devised during *March of the Falsettos*: he plotted most of the story himself and then asked Finn to compose the songs. Lapine has confirmed his role in this partnership: "My strong suit is structure. That's what I bring to the table. I contribute to storyline and character. I give [Finn] feedback and sometimes ask him to write a new song. But he writes all the words and music."[70] An example that illustrates their collaboration in

---

[68] Terry Helbing, "A Glorious 'March'," *New York Native*, August 10, 1981.

[69] Bell, *Broadway Stories*, 19.

[70] Quoted in Steve Cohen, "The Finite Joy of William Finn," *Total Theater*, www.totaltheater.com /?q=node/364.

Falsettoland is the racquetball scene that occurs in the middle of the song "A Day in Falsettoland." Lapine created and even staged the racquetball game first and subsequently asked Finn to write music to accompany it.[71] Finn reused the staccato ostinato that represented Trina chopping vegetables in "This Had Better Come to a Stop" in *March of the Falsettos* to now represent the ricocheting of the ball in Marvin and Whizzer's game. Another example is the opening number, "Falsettoland." Finn wrote several short musical excerpts to reintroduce the characters, but it was Lapine and musical director and orchestrator Michael Starobin who put them together to form a self-contained opening number.[72] Lapine's storytelling skills combined with Finn's songwriting craftsmanship created a "kaleidoscopic world of comedy and heartbreak with only seven performers."[73]

Falsettos

Falsettos was the title given to the double bill of *March of the Falsettos* and *Falsettoland*, which became, respectively, Acts I and II of a sung-through musical that tells Marvin's story from divorcing Trina to the loss of his new lover to AIDS. After *Falsettoland* closed in January 1991, Playwrights Horizons said that they did not have the funds to produce the two one-act musicals as a double bill. Mark Lamos from Hartford Stage in Connecticut, however, offered director Graciela Daniele the opportunity to direct the double bill for them that fall. After *The New York Times* praised it, Lincoln Center contemplated producing it. The deal fell through, and Finn sought out producers Barry and Fran Weissler, who had been courting him with other offers.[74] The Weisslers had seen *Falsettoland* at the Lucile Lortel and agreed to stage the double bill on Broadway with much of the original company under Lapine's direction. *Falsettos* opened at the John Golden Theatre on April 29, 1992, and closed on June 27, 1993, after 487 performances. Finn and Lapine won the Tony Award for best original book of a musical, and Finn won a Tony Award for best original score.

The double bill did not bring many changes to either *March of the Falsettos* or *Falsettoland*. Both musicals maintained the same structures that they had in their respective Off-Broadway productions, although Lapine made changes to

---

[71] William Finn, interview by author, New York, June 8, 2015.

[72] Finn, interview by author, May 21, 2013. I discuss the inception of *Falsettoland* and the songs in detail in Alex Bádue, "Performing Gender, Sexuality, and Jewishness in the Songs of William Finn's Musical *Falsettoland* (1990)," *Studies in American Jewish Literature* 38, no. 2 (2019): 159–78.

[73] Frank Rich, "What Has AIDS Done to Land of 'Falsettos'?" *New York Times*, June 29, 1990.

[74] For an account on why the Lincoln Center deal fell through, see Bell, *Broadway Stories*, 28–29.

their stagings. *March of the Falsettos* now included a new song, "I'm Breaking Down," borrowed from the 1981 revival of *In Trousers*, to provide Trina with a solo scene in which she reacts to her husband leaving her for another man. *Falsettos* made musical theater history because of its subject matter and structure. In a decade when sung-through musicals were strongly associated with the British counterparts (*Cats*, *Les Misérables*, *The Phantom of the Opera*, and *Miss Saigon*), Frank Rich praised *Falsettos* for being part of a theater season "marked by signs of an American musical renaissance on Broadway" and "a show in which the boundary separating Off Broadway and Broadway is obliterated."[75]

A New Brain

Finn and Lapine's next partnership also organizes the dramatic action from song to song. Similar to the Marvin musicals, *A New Brain* originated in songs, not from a book with spoken dialogue. In mid-1992, some months after he had won the two Tony Awards for *Falsettos*, Finn found out that he had something blocking the flow of fluid in his brain, causing it to accumulate in his skull. The first consultations revealed that he had an inoperable brain tumor. After some of the fluid was drained, he went through resonance tests that revealed that half of his brain was paralyzed. Although he did not have a tumor, Finn was diagnosed with an arteriovenous malformation (AVM), which occurs when blood from an artery flows directly into a vein, creating a mass of tissue that was blocking the fluid in his brain. Before Finn went through radiation to unblock the vein, the AVM hemorrhaged. Finn was bedridden for several weeks, and steroids made him hallucinate. By the end of 1992, he had undergone radiation, which resolved the AVM. The paralysis slowly weakened, and the songwriter started to recover.

This experience changed how Finn perceived the world and his own career. The years that followed were full of "unprecedented serenity . . . this was the time that I felt I had the new brain . . . a new way of thinking. Simplifying, not being cynical."[76] Finn had a burst of creativity during his recuperation process and wrote about his life-changing experience in the form of songs. He remembered:

> When I came out of the hospital, I couldn't sit at the piano without writing a decent song. At the piano, there was just all this gratitude that I was alive and all this life spewing out of me – the piano was singing – and I was just

---

[75] Frank Rich, "Broadway Boundary Falls Amid Reunions," *New York Times*, April 30, 1992.
[76] Quoted in Ellen Pall, "The Long-Running Musical of William Finn's Life," *New York Times*, June 14, 1998.

there to write it down. And so I had a bunch of these songs and I started putting them together, making a show.[77]

He composed the songs contemplating a possible revue:

> All the songs were written for the show, I worked on them for five years [1993–1998]. It was a very difficult time for me, and I was writing the story of my life. My first night out of the hospital, I knew how to write it [the song "I Feel So Much Spring"], what each verse was going to do. I had been diagnosed with a life-threatening disease. It was difficult! I like to express pain and joy at the same time in my songs, and first night out of the hospital, I finally knew how to write it.[78]

It was director and choreographer Graciela Daniele who, after listening to the songs, suggested that a revue would not be sufficient to depict a life experience of this magnitude.[79]

Finn initially wrote eight songs that formed the basis of *A New Brain*. These included "I Feel So Much Spring," "And They're Off," "I'd Rather Be Sailing," and "The Music Still Plays On."[80] After some time working on the material, Daniele and Finn decided that they needed Lapine's help to conceive a plot that would connect the songs in coherent dramaturgy. Lapine joined the creative team after the musical had had some workshop performances and, contrary to the usual practice in musical theater, helped Finn conceive a book out of songs. Lapine also created the character of Mr. Bungee (the protagonist's boss) and made the medical information less literal and more comical. Just like they had done in the 1980s, Lapine would tell Finn what type of song was needed, especially those concerning Mr. Bungee. Lapine stated his view on *A New Brain*: "If you try to articulate what the show's about, it's so clichéd. Smell the flowers. But what makes it unique is that it is told through Bill's voice."[81]

A New Brain tells the story of Gordon, a composer who writes music for a TV show hosted by Mr. Bungee. Gordon is very dissatisfied with his job and the types of songs he is required to compose. After he is diagnosed with AVM and requires surgery, the musical explores Gordon's relationship with his friend (Rhoda), mother, and boyfriend (Roger). Gordon's mother throws all of his books away, and a homeless lady, who appears throughout the musical begging for change, finds and starts selling them. After Gordon survives the surgery, he

---

[77] Interview with William Finn and Malcolm Getts in "What Musicals Are All About," *Lincoln Center Theater Review* 18 (Spring 1998): 16.

[78] Finn, interview by author, June 8, 2015.

[79] Pall, "The Long-Running Musical of William Finn's Life."

[80] Finn, interview by author, June 8, 2015. In the same interview, Finn related that the song "Anytime (I Am There)" from his song cycle *Elegies* (2003) was originally composed for *A New Brain*, but eventually cut.

[81] Quoted in Pall, "The Long-Running Musical of William Finn's Life."

sees the homeless lady, who insists on charging him for the books. Gordon concedes not to have the books back and takes the opportunity to make other changes and start a new phase of his life.

A New Brain opened Off-Broadway at the Mitzi E. Newhouse Theater at Lincoln Center on June 18, 1998, and closed on October 11, after a couple of extensions in the run and cast replacements. Several of the critics commented on the work's sung-through structure. Charles Isherwood wrote, "Despite being virtually sung-through – or indeed perhaps because of it – [the musical] seems more a disconnected series of numbers strung together than a shapely told tale."[82] Sam Whitehead wrote that the book for this musical "can be described only as thin to nonexistent,"[83] revealing that Finn again effaced the lines between book and lyrics. For her part, Daniele embraced and directed the show precisely because of its unconventional structure: "The challenge mostly is not [the musical's] theme. It's the fact that the piece is very impressionistic. It is not a conventional musical with a plot and a book and numbers. It's like a cycle of songs, with a very strong thematic line and a slight plot."[84]

Gay-Jewish Representation in Finn's Musical Theater

In addition to their sung-through structures, these musicals by Finn occupy an important place in American theater history because of the way they represent gay-Jewish men. Jonathan Friedman writes that before and even in the years following Stonewall, gay-Jewish characters "had no other alternative but to choose the way of the closet," although the representation of heterosexual Jewish men was becoming more positive.[85] The decades following Stonewall saw plays that deepened characterization, life experiences, and psychological conflicts of gay-Jewish male characters, such as Martin Sherman's *Bent* (1979) and Harvey Fierstein's *Torch Song Trilogy* (1981). *In Trousers* and *March of the Falsettos* came out in the same period and prompted musical theater's participation in this new, more realistic form of representation. *Falsettoland* went even further by not just presenting humanized and non-stereotypical gay characters but also educating the audience about life with AIDS, following a trend observed in plays like Larry Kramer's *The Normal Heart* and William M. Hoffman's *As Is*, both of which premiered in 1985. In Finn's two Broadway musicals of the 1990s, *Falsettos* and *A New Brain*, the gay characters' identity is a given and not the source of their dramas.

---

[82] Charles Isherwood, "Off-Broadway: *A New Brain*," *Variety*, June 22, 1998.

[83] Sam Whitehead, "Reviews: *A New Brain*," *Time Out New York*, June 25, 1998.

[84] Quoted in Allan Wallach, "Second Chances: An Artist's Musical Journey through Illness," *Newsday*, June 16, 1998.

[85] Jonathan C. Friedman, *Rainbow Jews: Jewish and Gay Identity in the Performing Arts* (Lanham, MD: Lexington Books, 2007), 49.

Post-Stonewall musical theater was not entirely vocal or even willing to challenge gay and Jewish representations until Finn's musicals. Stephen Sondheim, who like Finn was Jewish and gay, was conspicuously cautious about these themes in his works, especially in *Company* (1970) and *Follies* (1971). Gay characters in musicals of the 1970s include Sebastian Baye in *Coco* (1969),[86] Duane in *Applause* (1970), David in *Seesaw* (1973), and Paul in *A Chorus Line* (1975), but they were small parts and/or undermined by the end of the story. Perhaps the greatest break of musical theater's silence toward representation of gay (but not Jewish) characters came with Jerry Herman's *La Cage aux Folles* (1983), whose songs "I Am What I Am" and "The Best of Times" became hymns of the gay community in the 1980s. However, as John Clum has argued, Albin's drag into Zaza reinforces the stereotype of the effeminate gay man (who has to be fixed and taught into "Masculinity," as one song goes) and makes homosexuality safe, as Georges and Albin (as Zaza) act as a heterosexual couple.[87]

Finn's sung-through musicals portray gay-Jewish men whose dramas and conflicts transcend these identities and deal with psychological and emotional implications of living with serious health issues, like AIDS and AVM. Thus, Finn opened a door in musical theater that allowed the creation and acceptance of gay characters, like Molina in *Kiss of the Spider Woman* (1993); Tom Collins, Angel, and Joanne in *Rent* (1996); Alfie in *A Man of No Importance* (2002); Alison in *Fun Home* (2013); and Prince Charming in Lloyd Webber, Emerald Ferrell, and David Zippel's *Cinderella* (2021). To boot, challenging the representation of Jewish gay men came accompanied by defying the means through which music develops both the characters and the dramatic action. In the same way that the characters transcend stereotypical representations, they transcend spoken language and act out their stories solely in song. Unintentional as the sung-through format was in Finn's creative and compositional processes, it introduces particular characters, situations, and representations through an unusual form of musical theater presentation. Finn confirmed the pleasure of experiencing the world in song: "I think that what music and great lyrics can do is make life richer. You take a moment from life and you don't know it's great, you don't know it's as special as it is. Then you hear it sung and all of a sudden you have goosebumps and everything seems to have changed and the world seems different."[88]

---

[86] *Coco* opened in December 1969, six months after the Stonewall riots. Rene Auberjonois, who played Sebastian, won the Tony Award for best featured actor, the first for an actor playing a gay character.

[87] John Clum, *Still Acting Gay: Male Homosexuality in Modern Drama*, Revised ed. (New York: Palgrave Macmillan, 2000), 28–31.

[88] William Finn, "According to Finn: Song Notes Written by William Finn," an insert accompanying the Playbill for the Off-Broadway musical *Make Me a Song* at New World Stages (*Playbill* 123, no. 11 [November 2007]).

4 Nearly Sung-Through

On February 26, 1996, a month after Jonathan Larson's (1960–1996) tragic death immediately before *Rent*'s Off-Broadway dress rehearsals began, drama critic John Heilpern wrote about his experience seeing *Rent*: "Blasted by sung-through rock, I find myself looking to the great tradition of the American musical, rooted in the perfect, balanced synthesis of score, narrative, and dance. The form and discipline of Rodgers and Hammerstein's *Carousel* isn't a bad premise at all for the most ultramodern of musicals – if only to reverse all the rules."[89] Despite pointing out what he thought were some of the flaws in Larson's musical, Heilpern's review validated how *Rent* broke new ground not just because it portrayed and celebrated life and death in downtown New York City during the AIDS crisis but also because it unquestionably reversed "rules," or conventions, of musical theater composition.

Rent's musical structure does not comply with the form of Rodgers and Hammerstein, it does not follow the sung-through format of the British shows, nor does it continue the approaches observed in *The Human Comedy* or Finn's musicals. Larson's seven-year compositional process resulted in a musical that is best characterized as nearly sung-through. Songs occupy a center position in every scene and are circumscribed with patter (or recitative), underscoring, or snippets of spoken dialogue. Thus, music and singing outweigh spoken passages, and the demarcation between the two is not as clearly defined as it is in a conventional book musical, nor is it completely gone as in a thoroughly sung-through score.

This approach is of course not new. The idea of nearly sung-through occurs in book musicals but usually only within the scope of a single number (or scene) in which music dominates and short spoken passages connect the musical ones. Examples include the bench scene in *Carousel* (1945), "Tradition" in *Fiddler on the Roof* (1964), "Simple" in *Anyone Can Whistle* (1964), and the prologue of *Into the Woods* (1987). Frank Loesser's *The Most Happy Fella* (1956) made history for its sheer amount of music, which gives the impression of the musical being sung-through, although some of its important scenes transpire in spoken dialogue. Why did the creators of nearly sung-through musicals adhere to this format in the 1990s and at the turn of the twenty-first century? During a time when the vast majority of musicals succeeding on and off Broadway were traditional book musicals and entirely sung-through (especially British) musicals continued to be popular, why did some creative teams opt for something in between? What were their dramatic and aesthetic goals? How did they decide

---

[89] John Heilpern, "*Rent*: Glorious Last Testament Shakes Up the American Musical," *New York Observer*, February 26, 1996.

what was to be sung and what was to be spoken? What functions do short spoken passages acquire? Finally, what contributions and impact did these choices bring to the development of musical theater at the end of the twentieth century and toward the new millennium?

Michael John LaChiusa's *Hello Again* (1993)

The nearly sung-through structures in several of the musicals by Michael John LaChiusa (b. 1962) result from the composer's intent to create ambiguity between singing and speaking. In an essay for *The New York Times*, he explained: "I like to keep an audience guessing. A character might sing a line, speak the next, sing the next five, then deliver a spoken monologue and then the number. I'll probably go to musical hell for it."[90] This ambiguity defines how audiences experience musical theater: "It causes great anxiety in the audience so that you have a long stretch of music or long, long stretch of dialogue. It tricks the ear, tricks the emotional template, subconsciously, for the audience . . . they feel [the musical] as a living thing."[91] Playing with the audience's expectation helps LaChiusa shape a musical and decide what is to be sung and what is to be spoken: "You have to be choosy about what's sung, what's not sung. It might not be clear, but there is definitely a reason why something sounds something. And it's not always a matter of importance, [but] it's a matter of emotion."[92] LaChiusa's first commercially successful musical, *First Lady Suite* (1993), was a nearly sung-through musical that effaced the lines between speaking and singing. Other examples include *Hello Again* (1993), *Marie Christine* (1999), *Little Fish* (2003), *See What I Wanna See* (2005), *Bernarda Alba* (2006), and *First Daughter Suite* (2015).[93]

Based on Arthur Schnitzler's 1897 play *La Ronde*, *Hello Again* dramatizes ten characters who pair up for sexual encounters in ten different scenes. A character from one scene moves on to the next, breaking up with the old partner in favor of a new one. LaChiusa added to Schnitzler's plot by setting each scene in a different decade of the twentieth century. Scene 1 shows a sexual encounter between the Whore and the Soldier circa 1900, Scene 2 the Soldier and the Nurse in the 1940s, Scene 3 the Nurse and the College Boy in the 1960s, Scene 4 the College Boy and the Young Wife at the movies in the 1930s, Scene 5

---

[90] Michael John LaChiusa, "I Sing of America's Mongrel Culture," *New York Times*, November 14, 1999.

[91] Michael John LaChiusa, interview by author, New York, June 22, 2015.

[92] Michael John LaChiusa, interview by author, June 22, 2015.

[93] I provide a detailed analysis of five of LaChiusa's sung-through scores in Alex Bádue, "The Sung and the Spoken in Michael John LaChiusa's Musicals," in *Routledge Companion to the Contemporary Musical*, ed. Jessica Sternfeld and Elizabeth Wollman (New York: Routledge, 2020), 97–105.

the Young Wife and her Husband in the 1950s, Scene 6 the Husband and the Young Thing (a young adult in his twenties) aboard the Titanic in 1912, Scene 7 the Young Thing and the Writer in the 1970s, Scene 8 the Writer and the Actress in the 1920s, Scene 9 the Actress and the Senator in the 1980s, and the last scene (Scene 10) the Senator in the 1990s with the Whore of Scene 1. LaChiusa discarded chronological order, and the music, through pastiche, provides hints to help the audience identify the decade in which each scene takes place.

Three techniques that LaChiusa employed in *Hello Again* reveal how he succeeded in creating a nearly sung-through musical that fulfilled his aesthetic goals. First, he structures scenes around a single song that, although interrupted by underscoring, recitatives, and spoken lines, is prolonged as the dramatic action unfolds. Second, he incorporates song excerpts that are neither fully developed songs with structural closure nor reprises to create sound pastiches particular to each decade. Third, he uses musical recurrences to create continuity across multiple scenes.

The first scene offers a clear example of the first technique, creating a scene around a song. Here, the Whore seduces the Soldier with the title song, "Hello Again." The song is in a standard AABA form followed by a dance break and a final iteration of the A section. The Whore sings the principal strains, while the Soldier interrupts her with spoken interjections and recitatives. He initially rejects her but slowly becomes unable to resist her seduction (see Table 1).

The Soldier's recitatives, which employ a narrow vocal range and repeated pitches that contrast with the Whore's tuneful waltz, are fragments of his own song, "I Got a Little Time," with which he seduces the Nurse in the following scene. In addition, in A3 LaChiusa alters the melody when the Whore sings "we may die tomorrow" and successfully seduces the Soldier. The same occurs in A4 after the dance break on the words "how about a dime, love?" The music that once formed the climax of her seduction now sees her in a humiliating situation. A4 also includes a short spoken passage above an instrumental version of the song's main theme in which the Whore reveals her name to the Soldier. At the scene's end, a chordal arpeggiation underscores her realization that the Soldier stole her brooch.

In addition to structuring each scene around a single song, LaChiusa also employs song excerpts in passages that mix underscoring, recitative, and spoken dialogue. This happens in scenes 2, 5, 6, and 9. These excerpts do not derive from other songs (therefore, they are not reprises), nor do they develop into full-fledged songs or find musical closure. They are always sung by characters other than the scene's main couple, and their musical style establishes the time period. Their structural roles are identical: they segue into dialogue (both sung and spoken), which then segues into the main song of the scene (see Table 2).

Table 1 Form and structure of the song "Hello Again"

Section	Measure numbers	Comments
A1	mm. 1–38	Soldier interjects spoken lines (mm. 15–16 and mm. 24)
Soldier's recitative	mm. 38–45	
A2	mm. 46–74	Soldier interjects spoken lines (mm. 52–53) and a sung line (mm. 60–61)
Soldier's recitative	mm. 74–81	
B	mm. 82–103	
Soldier's recitative	mm. 99–110	
A3	mm. 111–48	Soldier sings one line (mm. 117–18) and speaks another (mm. 124–25)
Dance break	mm. 149–200	
A4	mm. 201–54	

"Zei Gezent" evokes the 1940s in what LaChiusa calls a "song of war-time best wishes,"[94] while "At the Prom" introduces the 1950s as "a young Neil Sedaka-type pop singer performs."[95] The latter occurs diegetically as the Young Wife listens to the radio. The Husband enters and switches stations, cutting the song off and choosing instead "something operatic," the song "Maien Zeit."[96] The same excerpted "Maien Zeit" returns at the beginning of Scene 6. In Scene 5, it characterizes the Husband as an upper-middle-class man who prefers opera to a popular song, whereas in Scene 6, it suggests "a first-class stateroom on a luxury liner."[97] The two excerpts that open Scene 9 are also diegetic, for they appear in 1980s pop-rock music videos that "the company … watches … using remotes to switch channels."[98]

Although none of the song excerpts find musical closure, LaChiusa maintains continuous musical underscoring, with some vocal lines sung and other spoken, as the couples discuss their relationships. Musical themes in conjunction with spoken lines link the excerpts to the full-blown songs. For example, in Scene 5, the dialogue between the Young Wife and the Husband includes a new sung theme that sets the words "the greatest of adventures which a man and woman share is marriage."[99] In the song "Tom," the Young Wife intones this same

---

[94] Michael John LaChiusa, *Hello Again: A Musical* (New York: Dramatists Play Service, 1995), 11.
[95] LaChiusa, *Hello Again*, 37.   [96] LaChiusa, *Hello Again*, 37.
[97] LaChiusa, *Hello Again*, 45.   [98] LaChiusa, *Hello Again*, 63.
[99] LaChiusa, *Hello Again*, 42.

Table 2 Song excerpts in *Hello Again*

	Song excerpt		Song
Scene 2 (1940s):	"Zei Gezent"	*segues to* Sung/spoken dialogue *segues to*	"I Got a Little Time"
Scene 5 (1950s):	"At the Prom" + "Maien Zeit"	*segues to* Sung/spoken dialogue *segues to*	"Tom"
Scene 6 (1910s):	"Maien Zeit"	*segues to* Sung/spoken dialogue *segues to*	"Listen to the Music"
Scene 9 (1980s):	"Rock with Rock" + "Angel of Mercy"	*segues to* Sung/spoken dialogue *segues to*	"Mistress of the Senator"

theme and partial lyric when she sings that this man called Tom, whom she fantasizes, marks "the greatest of adventures of my life."[100]

An example of the third technique, the use of musical recurrence across scenes, is evident in Scene 6. The dialogue passage between the Husband and the Young Thing, which is both spoken and sung, can be divided into two subsections: first comes a waltz, which introduces the characters, and then a barcarolle, when they get to know each other better. This passage then leads to the seduction song, "Listen to the Music." To create musical unity, the "adventures" theme from Scene 5 is brought back in the dialogue passage. In the waltz section, the Young Thing speaks the line, "I remember what you taught me" and then sings the theme to the words, "lift the wine glass slowly as you bring it to your lips."[101] The same theme that the Husband used to instruct his wife on marital responsibilities now appears as he seduces a younger man. The theme returns during the barcarole after the Young Thing asks the Husband to tell him his wife's name. The Husband answers, "Emily," and sings to the same music the exact words about marriage that he sang with the Wife but with some rhythmic changes. In Scene 5, the text was set as steady eighth notes, but at this moment in Scene 6, some of the words are set to sixteenth notes, implying that the Husband is singing it in a hurry and dismissing all thoughts of his wife before committing adultery.

LaChiusa's choice for the nearly sung-through format proves his opinions on the state of the American musical at the turn of the twenty-first century. For him, the American musical had reached a point from which it had not continued to grow. He claimed that musicals became copies of old formulae, especially the book musical, and basically kept reinventing musical comedy. Although he acknowledged that some musicals pushed the genre forward, like *Rent* and *The Light in the Piazza* (2005), he characterized the greatest hits of the era as what he terms faux musicals, works "based on formulae" and in which "all sense of invention and craft is abandoned in favor of delivering what the audience thinks a musical should deliver . . . There is no challenge, no confrontation, no art."[102] He includes *The Producers* (2001), *Hairspray* (2002), and several jukebox musicals in this category. While his ideas and statements are thought-provoking and debatable, they do explain why LaChiusa opted to challenge conventions of the book musical. Since he described faux musicals as "mechanical" with "no room for risk, derring-do innovation,"[103] his own compositional techniques could not adhere too closely to this aesthetic but rather had to utilize and reshape it.

---

[100] LaChiusa, *Hello Again*, 44.   [101] LaChiusa, *Hello Again*, 46.

[102] Michael John LaChiusa, "The Great Gray Way," *Opera News* 70, no. 2 (August 2005): 33.

[103] LaChiusa, "The Great Gray Way," 33

The Case of *Rent*

The nearly sung-through structure of *Rent* resulted in part from Larson following an operatic model, Puccini's *La Bohème*. The original idea was to update the opera to the twentieth century after playwright Billy Aronson saw a production of it at the Met and realized that the struggles, poverty, and disease-ridden lives of the young artistic characters in the opera could resonate with many residents of New York City in the late 1980s. *Rent* follows a year in the life of eight young bohemian artists struggling to overcome poverty and deal with physical and emotional complications in the age of AIDS (four of them have HIV). The musical treats serious themes such as gender identity, infidelity, and death as the protagonists fight to have their bohemian ideals seen and heard through their art, whether it is music, film, dance, theater, or fashion.

Aronson began working on the project in 1988 and contacted Playwrights Horizons about finding a composer. He was given two names, one of which was Larson's.[104] After Aronson dropped out of the project in 1991, Larson continued it on his own. He looked to Henri Murger's book *Scènes de la vie de bohème*, on which *La Bohème* is based, and the opera itself to create his version of the story. Michael Greif, who directed the original production, confirms that the sung-through opera served as the model for *Rent*:

> Jonathan was a very dedicated student of Broadway musicals, and I think one of the reasons why it worked uptown [on Broadway] was because it is such a good blend of his love for traditional musical forms and his loyalty to *La Bohème* as a structure, which is a structure we all know works as a musical, as an operatic form, and then some of his adventure-ness as a composer and also as a thinker.[105]

In the same interview, Greif recalls how he and Larson constantly discussed how the musical was similar to and different from *La Bohème*. Greif explains that his job was "to know the [opera's] libretto as little as possible to make sure the events, the plot, the passions, the personal costs of *Rent* were not dependent on a working knowledge of *La Bohème*. But I think [Larson] loved the fact that he was going back, harking back to that kind of classical form."[106]

Aronson's first drafts of the plot were not in a sung-through format. He wrote the story as a play to which Larson inserted song lyrics. This followed a typical convention in musical theater writing: creating songs that come out of a play to

---

[104] Evelyn McDonnell and Kathy Silberger, *Rent by Jonathan Larson* (New York: Harper Entertainment, 1997), 18.

[105] Interview with Michael Greif: Raw Footage, videotaped in New York City on August 26, 2003, VHS NCOX 2166, directed by Michael Kantor, New York Public Library for the Performing Arts, Billy Rose Theatre Division, Theatre on Film and Tape Archive, New York.

[106] Michael Greif: Raw Footage, videotaped in New York City, August 26, 2003.

expand character, time, and place. Larson composed *Rent*'s three first songs, "Rent," "Santa Fe," and "I Should Tell You," according to this paradigm, and they remained in every version of the script until the final one. After Aronson's departure, Larson chose not to partner with another playwright, and as a songwriter himself, he composed new songs to expand characters and dramatic situations, fill plot gaps, and connect existing songs.[107] Like Finn's compositional process for the Marvin musicals, the fact that many portions of *Rent* move from song to song was a consequence, not an intention.

Rent features some spoken passages that, as in a traditional book musical, prepare the drama for the songs. However, these are not long and developed dialogues in the Rodgers and Hammerstein tradition. Rather, these are scattered short spoken passages that never dominate in any scene and leave the dramatic heavy lifting for the songs. The band underscores the vast majority of these passages, resulting in a nearly sung-through musical. For example, the musical's opening alternates between spoken and sung passages to introduce two of the main characters – Mark and Roger – and build drama that leads to the opening number, "Rent." This song, in turn, becomes the main structure for the rest of the scene and like "Hello Again" in LaChiusa's musical introduces other characters with a mix of sung and recitative passages.

Another example is the many vamps in the score. These short musical passages repeat in a loop and borrow riffs, themes, or the bass line of the songs. As they underscore snippets of spoken dialogue between songs, they become conduits of the dramatic action. For example, in Act II, the opening guitar riff of "Without You" underscores a brief dialogue between Roger and Mimi and conducts the action from the previous song, "Seasons of Love B," to "Without You." The opening riff of "I'll Cover You" does the same for Collins and Angel between "Santa Fe" and "I'll Cover You" (in Act I). Also in Act II, high hats and a bass drum underscore the dialogue about the expenses for Angel's funeral and become the intro to "What You Own." For these two last examples, Larson entered the spoken dialogue metrically in the music, with the rhythm notated in unheightened pitch, which one critic characterized as "a sort of grunge recitative."[108]

---

[107] Although Larson never partnered with another playwright, the producers hired playwright Lynn Thompson in 1995 to help and advise Larson.

[108] Eric Grode, "Review of *Rent*," *Backstage*, February 23, 1996. The dialogue concerning the payment for Angel's funeral was rapped during the Off-Broadway run in early 1996. After the musical moved to Broadway in April, the rhythmic accompaniment was maintained, but the words were spoken. Jonathan Larson, *Rent* played at the New York Theatre Workshop, January 26–March 31, 1996, prior to moving to Broadway, DVD NCOV 1915, New York Public Library for the Performing Arts, Billy Rose Theatre Division, and Theatre on Film and Tape Archive, New York.

Rent's underscored spoken passages or even without music take on specific dramaturgical goals. Among these are Mark's narrative intermediations that announce the location for some scenes and provide background information on certain characters, such as when he introduces Collins before "Today 4 U," and when he introduces Benny at the beginning of "You'll See." These intermediations and indeed Mark's role as a sort of narrator did not enter the script until after Larson's death. Greif added them to facilitate the transitions from one song to another. He based them on a version of *Rent* that had been workshopped the previous year and noted that "the language for those additions was taken from stage directions and character biographies [that] Larson had written."[109]

Joanne and Maureen's scene after "Happy New Year B" offers an example of unaccompanied spoken dialogue. The couple is rehearsing Maureen's new protest and cannot agree on how she should perform it. This dialogue segues to them singing about their personality differences in the duet "Take Me or Leave Me." This song was one of the last to be added to the musical and probably the last song Larson ever composed. Larson's sketch for the lyrics is dated January 1, 1996,[110] and the song's title appears for the first time in a song list that Larson compiled on January 11, 1996.[111] A script dated January 16, 1996, nine days before previews were scheduled to begin, is the first to plot "Take Me or Leave Me."[112] Unaccompanied dialogue was probably deemed the only way to introduce the new song into the already established dramatic action.

In book musicals, songs typically start when speaking is no longer adequate for expression or characterization. The opposite happens in *Rent*. When characters can no longer convey their thoughts through song, they start to speak. One example is Maureen's protest number against gentrification in the Lower East Side, "Over the Moon." The song's placement between non-diegetic songs, "Christmas Bells" and "La Vie Bohème," and the fact that the number blends singing with unaccompanied speech accentuate the power of the spoken word in Maureen's protest. Another example in which singing is not enough and the characters must resort to speaking includes the eulogies for Angel. Although they are accompanied by the opening riff of "Seasons of Love," Maureen, Mimi, and Mark speak their homage to Angel between two songs, "Contact"

---

[109] Evelyn McDonnell, "Not Just a Fable, a Testament: *Rent* Moves from Alphabet City to Broadway," *Village Voice*, April 30, 1996.

[110] Jonathan Larson, *Rent* Show Materials, "Script, 1/11/96, Notes, Lyric Sketches, etc.," Box 17, Folder 1, Jonathan Larson Papers, Music Division, Library of Congress, Washington, DC.

[111] Jonathan Larson, *Rent* Show Materials, "Miscellany," Box 17, Folder 4, Jonathan Larson Papers, Music Division, Library of Congress, Washington, DC.

[112] Jonathan Larson, *Rent* Show Materials, "Script, 1996 Jan. 16," Box 17, Folder 3, Jonathan Larson Papers, Music Division, Library of Congress, Washington, DC.

and a reprise of "I'll Cover You." This placement of speech between songs intensifies the dramatic impact of the eulogies.

With *Rent*, Larson demonstrated the possibilities of a nearly sung-through musical. While using techniques such as vamping to create continuous music, he also showed the dramatic force of carefully placed spoken passages, both with and without musical underscoring. After Larson's death, Sondheim said in an interview that Larson was one of the few theater composers "attempting to blend contemporary pop music with theater music" and was "on his way to finding a real synthesis." Sondheim concluded that a theater songwriter "must have a sense of what is theatrical, of how you use music to tell a story, as opposed to writing a song. Jonathan understood that instinctively."[113]

Andrew Lippa and the Turn of the Twenty-First Century

The nearly sung-through format appeared in several other examples of musicals from the late 1990s and early 2000s. A notable example is Andrew Lippa's (b. 1964) *The Wild Party* (2000). This is not to be confused with LaChiusa's *Wild Party*. Both composers based their musicals on Joseph Moncure March's 1928 eponymous narrative poem, and both musicals opened in the 1999–2000 season: Lippa's played Off-Broadway, and LaChiusa's on Broadway. The story, set in prohibition-era New York City, is about Queenie and Burrs, two vaudevillian actors whose marital crisis leads them to throw a party to hide and escape their problems. As the party unfolds, they become intricately entwined in the crisis of another couple, Kate and Black.

Lippa started out his project with the intention to create a sung-through piece. He did not write lyrics at the time, so he wanted to set March's entire poem to music, without altering the words. He purposefully intended this to be similar to Lloyd Webber's *Cats*, a musical structured by poems.[114] Henry Krieger's *Dreamgirls* (1981) was also an influence: "If *Dreamgirls* hadn't existed, *The Wild Party* would not exist. I wanted *The Wild Party* to move strictly when it came down to what it looked like, how it moved, how it was always dancing, to be like *Dreamgirls* in that respect."[115] As Lippa developed the project, he realized that such structure was not going to work. He explained: "The poem was almost exclusively third-person narrative, and I got weary of writing in the third person. I wanted to write 'I feel . . ., ' 'I am . . ., '"[116] so he decided to write the lyrics and book himself. Some passages

---

[113] Quoted in Anthony Tommasini, "A Composer's Death Echoes in His Musical," *New York Times*, February 11, 1996.

[114] Andrew Lippa, "An Interview with Andrew Lippa," *New York City Center Playbill*, July/August 2015, 20.

[115] Andrew Lippa, interview by author, New York, June 20, 2015.

[116] Lippa, "An Interview with Andrew Lippa," 20.

of the musical quote March's poem verbatim, but Lippa acknowledged that the source material slowly receded: "I suppose I used the poem most heavily for the first few scenes. You love source material when you find it, but sooner or later you have to trash it, you have to make it contemporary."[117]

This helped Lippa compose more songs. As he conceived passages to connect them and develop dramatic action, he was faced with the question of what should be sung and what should be spoken. He has argued: "So much of these things are just instinctual, and you just go. You go on based on what feels right as you're doing it, the choice is mainly instinctive."[118] One example is his use of underscoring and a mix of singing and speaking in Act I, Scene 3. He embeds the songs "He Was Calm" and "Poor Child" with well-defined self-contained sections that include some sung dialogues and some spoken with underscoring (see Table 3).

Lippa uses musical cues to structure the scene and blur the limits between singing and speaking. Underscoring #1 is divided into three parts: first a dialogue between Kate, Phil, Oscar, and Black (marked "ricky ticky tempo" on the score); the second a dialogue between Sam and Dolores (marked "Broadway 'Two'"), and the third a dialogue between Burrs and Kate (marked as "tempo di Look at Me Now," Kate's entrance song earlier in the scene). Underscoring #2 is divided into two parts: a dialogue between Nadine and Madelaine (the music foreshadows Madelaine's "Old-Fashioned Love Story" from the next scene) and a dialogue between Eddie, Mae, and Burrs (marked "tempo di Sweet Georgia Brown"). Underscoring #3 initially reduces musical accompaniment to long, sparse chords as Queenie and Black interact for the first time. As their flirting grows more overt, musical characteristics change and become accompaniment for the quartet "Poor Child." Through different musical styles and alternation between sung and spoken sections, Lippa introduces the audience to the eccentricities of the party's guests and the conflicts of the four protagonists. He repeats a similar structure in Act I, Scene 5 (when underscoring and few spoken passages embed the songs "The Juggernaut" and "Wild, Wild Party"), and Act II, Scene 2, when underscoring and short spoken passages embed the songs "Who Is This Man?" "The Gal for Me," "I'll Be There," and "Listen to Me."

Alongside LaChiusa, Larson, and Lippa, other musical theater composers played with the form and structure of the book musical in the 1990s and early 2000s and challenged the balance between singing and speaking. They represent the turn-of-the-century version of Loesser's statement regarding his *Most*

---

[117] Quoted in Brendan Lemon, "A Composer Unlocks the Lyricist within, Helped by a Hot Poem," *New York Times*, February 13, 2000.
[118] Lippa, interview by author, June 20, 2015.

Table 3 Embedment of songs in Act I, Scene 3, of *The Wild Party*

Music	Dramatic action
Song: "He Was Calm"	Queenie and the party guests observe Black
Underscoring #1	Spoken dialogue between party guests
Sung	Black observes the party
Underscoring #2	Spoken dialogue between party guests
Sung dialogue	Black and Kate sing about Queenie
Underscoring #3	Spoken dialogue between Black, Queenie, and Burrs, then Black and Kate
Song: "Poor Child"	The four protagonists sing about their feelings

Happy Fella: "[A] musical with a lot of music."[119] For example, Stephen Sondheim and James Lapine's *Passion* (1994) features music throughout its one-act structure and does not make room for audience applause. The continuous music morphs into and out of songs and becomes underscoring for spoken dialogue. Krieger's *Side Show* (1997) originally contained spoken dialogue by Bill Russell, who also wrote the lyrics to Krieger's music. It was not until later in the production, after music director David Chase started rehearsing the numbers, that the creators decided to musicalize Bill Russell's dialogues in recitative style. Krieger made use of motives and specific phrasings to musically connect a character's recitatives to his or her songs, resulting in a nearly sung-through musical.[120] The recitatives have proved to be challenging, and subsequent productions of *Side Show*, especially in regional theaters, dismissed them altogether and had the actors speaking the dialogue.

Some of the musicals by Stephen Flaherty and Lynn Ahrens also feature a great amount of continuous music that gives the impression of being nearly sung-through. *Ragtime* (1998) has several numbers that alternate between singing and speaking with underscoring, such as the prologue ("Ragtime") and "Journey On." It also features spoken narrative intermediations by several characters (often also with underscoring) and book scenes with spoken dialogue that culminate in song, such as Scene 2, which ends with "Goodbye, My Love." In *Seussical* (2000), the dramatic action moves from song to song with great amount of singing and metric rhyming spoken passages in the style of

---

[119] Quoted in Geoffrey Block, "Frank Loesser's Sketchbooks for 'The Most Happy Fella'," *Musical Quarterly* 73, no. 1 (1989): 6.

[120] David Chase, e-mail to author, January 29, 2014.

Dr. Seuss (some are actual passages from his books), some of which are underscored.

Nearly sung-through musicals mark a unique way through which the musical changed and reinvented itself in the 1990s and early 2000s. As it found a comfortable aesthetic place between the conventional book musical and the complete sung-through musical, it did shift "the perfect, balanced synthesis of score, narrative, and dance."[121] These shows represent a generation of composers, lyricists, and book writers that took the musical to the new century and millennium, proving that the same rules and conventions of the book musical had the potential to be adapted into something new.

5 "Maid for Broadway": The Sung-Through Structure of *Caroline, or Change*

The 2003–2004 Broadway season was a strong one for musical theater. It introduced the puppets from *Avenue Q*, a new perspective on L. Frank Baum's *The Wonderful Wizard of Oz* as seen from the perspective of the Wicked Witch of the West in *Wicked*, and Hugh Jackman's Tony-Award-winning performance as Peter Allen in *The Boy from Oz* (not the same Oz as in *Wicked*). The season also saw renowned musical theater names appear in revivals, such as Neil Patrick Harris and Michael Cerveris in *Assassins*, Alfred Molina as the beloved Tevye in *Fiddler on the Roof*, and Donna Murphy as Ruth in Leonard Bernstein's *Wonderful Town*. In the midst of these classics and soon-to-become classics, composer Jeanine Tesori (b. 1961) and playwright Tony Kushner (b. 1956) presented their sung-through musical *Caroline, or Change*, which may not have had the same commercial impact and success as *Avenue Q*, *Wicked*, and *The Boy from Oz*, but its score and text deliver important and topical messages, placing the sung-through musical vis-à-vis racial issues of the first two decades of the twenty-first century.[122]

Set in Lake Charles, Louisiana, in November 1963, the action centers on Caroline Thibodeaux, the African American maid of a white Jewish family, the Gellmans, and a struggling single mother making US $30 a week. As the plot unfolds, the musical explores the impact of JFK's assassination and the Civil Rights Movement on its characters. Caroline's friend, Dotty, and daughter, Emmie, embrace social changes for African American women of the time, while Caroline resists them. Noah, the boy in the Gellman household, idolizes

---

[121] Heilpern, "*Rent*: Glorious Last Testament Shakes Up the American Musical."

[122] After decades of British sung-through musicals coming to the USA, *Caroline, or Change* reversed the trend with a successful British revival that started at the Chichester Festival Theatre in 2017, then reprised in London's Hampstead Theatre in March 2018. It moved to the West End in December of that year.

Caroline and enjoys spending time with her in the basement. Noah's step-mother, Rose, gets annoyed that Noah leaves coins in his pockets and wants to teach him the importance of not wasting money. She tells Caroline to keep the change that Noah leaves in his pockets. Caroline first rejects the idea, but as she realizes that her own children need food and clothing, she concludes that some change can help. Noah realizes that by leaving the money in his pockets, he can help the Thibodeaux family and starts doing it on purpose. One day Noah forgets he had a US $20 bill in his pocket, and according to his stepmother's rules, if Caroline finds it, she can keep it. When Noah arrives home, he asks Caroline for the bill, and Caroline says that the money is hers now. They fight, and Caroline leaves the money in the bleach cup and refuses to go back to work. Dotty advises Caroline to finally catch up with the times and make a change in her life. Caroline finds herself caught between remaining a maid to a white family or embracing the social changes around her.

Kushner wrote *Caroline, or Change* in the 1990s, and it is to date his most autobiographical work. He, like Noah, grew up in Lake Charles, Louisiana, and was raised by an African American maid, Maudie Lee Davis.[123] The character Noah represents an amalgam of the playwright and his brother, Eric.[124] The play depicts aspects of Kushner's own childhood, and having come from a musical family (his father was a clarinetist and conductor; his mother played the bassoon and even recorded with Stravinsky in the 1950s), he wanted the music to occupy a vital part in the storytelling. He stated that "The fact that these characters would be singing gave it a non-naturalistic freedom that made it ok to address a subject like this."[125]

Kushner created the libretto for a San Francisco Opera commission, which partnered him with composer and jazz vocalist Bobby McFerrin. After McFerrin dropped out of the project, Kushner took his script to director George C. Wolfe, with whom he had worked previously on *Angels in America*, and Wolfe decided that it should be a musical and not an opera.[126] They wanted Tesori to compose the score, but it took them a year to convince her to join the project.[127] Tesori did not think that she was the right person to musicalize this story but recalled that after "talking to [Kushner] about his

---

[123] Simi Horwitz, "'Change' Panel: A Musical Raises Questions Not Easily Resolvable," *Backstage*, July 23, 2004. Davis's name is provided in Joe Dziemianowicz, "Maid for Broadway: Tony Kushner's Civil-Rights-Era Musical Moves Uptown," *Daily News*, April 25, 2004. I borrow Dziemianowicz's pun for the title of this section.

[124] Alex Abramovich, "Hurricane Kushner Hits the Heartland," *New York Times*, November 30, 2003.

[125] Jessica Branch, "Pastiche Perfect: Jeanine Tesori Juggles Musical Modes for *Caroline, or Change*," *Time Out New York*, November 20, 2003.

[126] Michael Giltz, "Tonya Meets Tony," *Advocate*, May 11, 2004.

[127] Harry Haun, "A Range of Change," *Playbill* 120, no. 5 (May 2004): 10.

intentions, I began to understand what he was after."[128] Another reason she was reluctant to join the creative team was that she did not "like just setting lyrics. I want to bring my own life experiences into play."[129] Kushner and Tesori had collaborated on a previous musical that never materialized, which proved that they could work together, and Kushner asked her to take another look at Caroline.[130]

After Tesori joined the creative team, the main structure of the book did not change: it remained as twelve scenes and an epilogue. *Caroline, or Change*'s sung-through structure came because Tesori received a fully completed script, which she was expected to set to music. The composer had dabbled with similar musical structures in *Violet* (1997) and would do so again in *Fun Home* (2013), but the experience with Kushner proved unique. She has recalled

> When we started out, [Kushner] thought this was a book musical. I said: "It's not a book musical. I don't know how I know that, I just know it." A lot of that stuff is really hard to verbalize because it's based on, you know, the inner pulse. . . . So we had a lot of talks about song form, rhythmic recitative, and that kind of stuff. And then we had to just make this story work with music. . . . I don't really have an intellectual reason for why [the musical is sung-through], except that it seemed likely to fit.[131]

As a result, Tesori's musical architecture allows characters to move in and out of songs through recitatives, ariosos, and ensemble passages, all of which exist within a musical continuum.

Tesori started by setting some of Kushner's words to music. Emmie's "I Hate the Bus" was the first music she composed for the musical.[132] As the project developed, she became involved in the writing and editing of the lyrics. Kushner had written a play in verse, and Tesori created ensemble numbers by overlapping existing lines and asking Kushner to craft new ones as needed. She musicalized scenes, created songs out of monologues, and devised means to connect the entire score together. She decided that some lines be spoken so that the contrast with singing could function the opposite way that it does in the book musical: "I think the speaking becomes the uncomfortable thing when most of it is sung. And it causes attention to itself."[133] (A similar process happens in *Rent*, as discussed in Section 3.) Tesori's craftsmanship allows the term opera to be used to describe the work, and even she herself referred to *Caroline* as "a

---

[128] Quoted in Blake Green, "Music Maker," *Newsday*, November 30, 2003.
[129] Quoted in Green, "Music Maker."
[130] Tony Kushner and Jeanine Tesori, *Caroline, or Change: A Musical* (New York: Theatre Communications, 2004), xii.
[131] Jeanine Tesori, interview by author, New York, June 15, 2015.
[132] Tesori, interview by author, June 15, 2015.   [133] Tesori, interview by author, June 15, 2015.

people's opera and a reflection of America at its best, with all its different sounds, expressing collective and private worlds."[134] Theater critics described it as a musical with a "deliberately fragmented sung-through score"[135] in which the songs are "seamlessly knit."[136]

The structure and soundscape of the musical also come from the cultural diversity inherent in the plot. Just as Kushner imagined a house with different floors (the basement – where Caroline works – the living room and kitchen on the ground floor, and the bedrooms on the second floor), Tesori created a score with different layers.[137] This refers to not just the many genres and styles that make up the score (which include blues, R&B, Motown, soul, klezmer, classical, opera, and Sondheimesque sung dialogue) but also layers within the continuous music, namely truly sung passages (both recitatives and full-blown songs) and short underscored spoken segments. Layers of musical pastiche enhance the means through which characters express what they experience both individually and collectively, and the score's continuous music facilitates smooth transitions among these characters' diverse perspectives related to race, social class, and religion.

The Score

Tesori employs various musical elements to bring out specific aspects of Kushner's libretto. These include recurring motifs used to connect dramatic themes across different scenes and a mixture of song, recitative, and spoken dialogue to emphasize certain lines of text.

One of the recurring motifs is introduced in the opening scene at Noah's entrance in "Noah Down the Stairs." The motif represents the relationship between Noah and Caroline and consists of an ascending minor third between two eighth notes followed by an ascending leap of a perfect fifth set to a quarter note. In Act I, Scene 5, the figure underscores the duet between Noah and Caroline that links two of Caroline's songs, "Gonna Pass Me a Law" and "Noah Go to Sleep." In the former song, Caroline (in her house) expresses how her life would be if she could make changes after JFK's death. A dialogue in recitative follows, in which Noah (in his bed) disrupts Caroline's thoughts by asking her to bid him goodnight and confessing that he likes her, despite her temper. The motif underscores Noah's lines throughout most of the sequence and effects the

[134] Quoted Horwitz, "'Change' Panel."
[135] Ben Brantley, "Outsiders Bond in a South of Roiling Change," *New York Times*, December 1, 2003.
[136] John Rockwell, "Beyond Singles and Concept Albums, Pop Yearns for a Long Form," *New York Times*, January 2, 2004.
[137] Tesori, interview by author, June 15, 2015.

segue to "Noah Go to Sleep," in which Caroline sings about the difficulties she faces in order to get her children what they need, including a place to live, food, and basic health care. She cannot escape that tending to Noah's well-being takes most of her time and prevents her from tending to her own children. As a comment on the discrepancy between white/middle-class and black/working-class experiences, the song would not have the same impact had Noah and his theme not connected her dreams and aspirations in the first song to her harsh reality in the second. The motif returns at the end of the musical, though transformed. The ascending perfect fifth is now replaced with a descending forth, confirming that a change has happened in their friendship. It is still there, but it is not the same as it was when the musical began.

Another dramatically significant motif is introduced in Act 1, Scene 6, with Noah's line "Caroline took my money home," which the boy sings when he intentionally starts leaving money in his pocket. Set all in eighth notes, the words "Caroline took my" occur in the same pitch; the word "money" occurs a minor third below; and "home" another whole step below. Tesori uses the theme to connect three of the songs that make up the scene, "Stuart and Noah," "Quarter in the Bleach Cup," and "Roosevelt Petrucius Coleslaw."

In "Stuart and Noah," Stuart (Noah's father) tells the boy that he will start receiving a weekly allowance, and Noah fantasizes about everything he can buy with the money. Meanwhile, Caroline realizes that the amount of money in the bleach cup is growing, and it could help her and her children. This segues to Noah – with his new allowance – leaving quarters on purpose for her. The musical accompaniment quotes the main theme of Mozart's Clarinet Concerto in A, indicating that Stuart – a clarinetist – is more preoccupied with practicing his clarinet than observing how Noah uses the money. At the end of the song, Caroline takes the money, and Noah introduces his musical theme, almost a capella, to the words "Caroline took my money home." The sparse chords of the three measures emphasize the words "Caroline," "money," and "home" and cue the opening of "Quarter in the Bleach Cup," in which Noah and Caroline sing about her taking his quarters home. When Noah purposefully leaves a dollar bill in his pants, Caroline thinks it is too much for her to take, and she speaks her lines to express this. Noah continues to leave quarters in his pants, but Caroline stops taking them and leaves them in the bleach cup. In the song's climax, she takes 75 cents home, singing to herself that "thirty dollars [a week] ain't enough."[138] Noah sings "Caroline takes my money home" to the theme described previously and imagines that he is now the topic of conversation at the Thibodeaux household. A strumming guitar vamp underscores

---

[138] Kushner and Tesori, *Caroline, or Change*, 56.

Caroline in her house calling her children, and when she gives each of them a quarter, the band plays Noah's theme.[139] Caroline has a recitative in which she tells the children that the money is theirs to keep. The strumming guitar returns and becomes the beginning of "Roosevelt Petrucius Coleslaw," in which the children dream of what they can buy with the money, while Noah continues to believe that he is their hero, singing variations of the "Caroline took my money home" theme. A particularly effective example of Tesori and Kushner's creative partnership is evident in this scene, for both plot and music dramatize how choices in one house affect the other. The Gellmans's reality – where change can be given away – is conflated with that of the Thibodeauxs, where quarters provide basic necessities. It is Noah's "Caroline took my money home" theme that links these two worlds.

Similar to LaChiusa, Tesori structures scenes that unevenly balance spoken and sung texts, along with recitative passages. The difference between speech and singing often indicates characters who are in disagreement – one speaks; the other sings. This is evident in Act 1, Scene 6, the same scene previously discussed. In the first song of the sequence, "Noah Has a Problem," Rose tells Caroline to keep the change that she finds in Noah's pocket, which Caroline refuses to do. Rose sings her lines, while Caroline speaks hers, revealing their discordance.

In Act II, Scene 9, after Noah realizes that Caroline is not going to return his US $20 bill, he sings: "President Johnson has built a bomb special made to kill all Negroes . . . I hope he drops his bomb on you."[140] Offended, Caroline speaks – not sings – her reply to Noah, in which she describes the temperature in hell. A sustained C in the bass slowly fades out, leaving the orchestra mute when she says, "Hell's so hot it makes flesh fry." Then, Caroline sings a cappella, the hurtful words, "And hell's where Jews go when they die."[141] She has become so angry and upset that she becomes paradoxically calm and sings this line. She speaks (with no accompaniment) her final lines to the boy, "take your twenty dollars, baby. So long, Noah, goodbye."[142] This transition between singing a cappella and speaking, which contrasts with the continuous singing and instrumental comple- ment that characterizes the musical, strikingly reveals that Caroline and Noah's friendship has reached an emotional impasse. As Tesori explains:

> She [Caroline] submerges in grounds beneath the sea level, and her desires and her wants, because that's what's required. And that's the tragedy. It came out of this coin, a coin being dropped, the smallest of things, and the relationship of something so intimate between an adult and a child is

---

[139] In the original production and orchestration, the theme was played by a solo clarinet, echoing the origin of the money: Stuart.

[140] Kushner and Tesori, *Caroline, or Change*, 104.

[141] Kushner and Tesori, *Caroline, or Change*, 104.

[142] Kushner and Tesori, *Caroline, or Change*, 104.

complicated by money and circumstance, in a country that's nothing to do and everything to do with that.[143]

The importance of Caroline's lines at this precise moment are accentuated through the style of their presentation.

Such contrast between speaking and singing also marks Caroline's final lines in the musical. Noah asks her if she misses sharing a cigarette. She first speaks, "You bet I do, Noah," and then sings, "you bet." Her change from speech to singing indicates the beginning of reconciliation with the singing Noah. She is returning to his mode of vocal expression.

Tesori sometimes expands the relationship between spoken and sung lines to include diegetic and non-diegetic functions of music. One instance of this occurs in the duet Caroline sings with her daughter, Emmie, in Act I, Scene 5. The song "No One Waitin'" is a diegetic blues song that the radio sings (the radio is embodied by three female singers in the style of The Supremes). At first, it underscores the spoken dialogue in which Caroline asks Emmie why she was away from home on the day that the president was assassinated. The radio's song comments on the dramatic action with lines like, "Nobody's arm to cradle my head, to talk about news, talk about views, talk about change, about the president's death."[144] When Emmie admits that she was actually having fun, the music changes: the tempo indication on the score reads "hullabaloo," and the music becomes non-diegetic. Emmie sings about the good time she had during the day and her lack of interest in mourning JFK. The radio singers, no longer performing a diegetic radio broadcast, accompany her as backing vocals. Emmie's statement that she has "no tears to shed for no dead white president"[145] brings back not just the bluesy music of "No One Waitin'" but also its diegetic function as background music for the mother–daughter dialogue. Now, Caroline sings her lines in recitative, while Emmie speaks hers, indicating their disagreement. By playing with the dramatic function of underscoring in this scene (sometimes diegetic, sometimes non-diegetic), Tesori takes the technique of mixing the spoken and the sung in the same scene to a level that exceeds that of the other sung-through musicals considered in this study.

"That Ol' Copper Nightmare Man": The Singing Statue and the Musical's Epilogue

The compositional process of *Caroline, or Change* included Tesori making changes to Kushner's book and lyrics and Kushner contributing to the

---

[143] Tesori, interview by author, June 15, 2015.
[144] Kushner and Tesori, *Caroline, or Change*, 41.
[145] Kushner and Tesori, *Caroline, or Change*, 43.

score.[146] Tesori has commented, "I've never just set something to music without altering some of the words. It has to be, to me, that beautiful back and forth of two writers saying, 'let me give you,' 'alright, let me change' ... 'ok, oh, edit that' ... and then suddenly, it inextricably ties."[147] This intimate and intricate partnership caused some portions of the musical to be especially challenging to create and develop. The musical's epilogue exemplifies this, and an account of its compositional process identifies how sung-through musicals are written and rewritten. Since its inception, the epilogue was always sung-through, but it started out with sung dialogues and ended up being structured entirely as a number for Caroline's children.

Several scenes in the musical highlight the relationship between Caroline and her daughter. In Scene 4, Dotty tells Caroline that a courthouse statue of a Confederate soldier – a symbol of white supremacy in the South – has been vandalized, and in Scene 8, Dotty reports to Emmie that the statue was found headless wrapped in a Confederate flag thrown in a bayou. Also, in Scene 8, Caroline gets angry with Emmie for interrupting the Gellmans's conversation during the Chanukah party and disagreeing with them over Martin Luther King Jr. ("Kitchen Fight"). After Caroline demands that Emmie go back to the kitchen, Emmie belittles her mother's subservience and sings that social change will bring her better material comfort than Caroline has had in her life ("I Hate the Bus"). The musical's epilogue, "Emmie's Dream," brings Emmie to the stage, and she reveals that she was part of the group that decapitated the statue. She also atones for what she said to her mother in Scene 8.

The epilogue went through several changes as Kushner and Tesori sought a dramatically satisfying version. From workshops to the Off-Broadway production and the Broadway run, the epilogue went from being a confrontation between Emmie and the statue to becoming a sung monologue in which she narrates the confrontation. In early drafts of the script, the statue's head came to life onstage and begged to be put back on its body. In this scenario, the statue's head reveals that Emmie is the one who had vandalized it and thrown it into the bayou. Emmie's response and refusal to obey the statue's head confirmed her understanding that times were changing:

> **EMMIE**
> Oh mister copper hidden head
> Things ain't been as right as this
> For years; and now it starts to spread
> Across the South, what was amiss
> Begins a metamorphosis,

---

[146] Tesori, interview by author, June 15, 2015.   [147] Tesori, interview by author, June 15, 2015.

A word I learnt that mean
It changing . . .
For what we done, I ain't the least bit sorry,
I just wish they hadn't found your body.[148]

After this proclamation, the statue left the stage, and Emmie and her two little brothers, Jackie and Joe, claimed themselves to be proud children of a maid who stood strong in difficult times so that they could have a future. This structure for the epilogue was present in a 1999 reading of the musical and remained in place until 2003, just months before the Off-Broadway opening. It was Tesori who suggested that the epilogue be musically and lyrically rewritten and that they cut the confrontation with the statue's head. She explained: It was a big mess. We didn't spend enough time on that, and then when we got to the end, we really saw her [Emmie] taking over, and it was really important that she'd come out in a Shakespearian way and said, "we have just one more thing, and then you can go home."[149]

A script dated September 16, 2003, reveals the changes made to the epilogue and how it was performed during the show's Off-Broadway run (November 30, 2003–February 1, 2004).[150] Kushner's stage directions reinforce the dramaturgical focus of the epilogue: "Emmie has appeared on the lawn in her nightgown. Caroline looks at her, then goes inside, giving her daughter the stage."[151] Emmie sings about being scared for keeping a secret and having disobeyed social order. She confesses to being part of the group that beheaded the statue: "Now something has changed at the courthouse downtown, and all because of what we did."[152] She also confesses that the reason she stayed at the courthouse after the head fell was because she had discovered that she was a brave person and attributed this quality to the strength of her mother. Reconciling herself to her mother, Emmie is happy that she herself made a change and can now tell Caroline what really happened. Jackie and Joe come onstage and ask Emmie to speak low because their mother is sleeping after a hard day of work. The three bring the musical to an end, emphasizing that while Caroline may not be able to embrace social changes, her children – the new generation – can do so because of her.

---

[148] Quoted in James Fisher, *The Theater of Tony Kushner: Living Past Hope* (New York: Routledge, 2001), 205.

[149] Tesori, interview by author, June 15, 2015.

[150] Tony Kushner and Jeanine Tesori, *Caroline, or Change*, Script NCOF+05-1, Performing Arts Research Collection – Theatre, New York Public Library for the Performing Arts, Billy Rose Theatre Division, New York. The content of this script is identical to the Off-Broadway performance that the New York Public Library for the Performing Arts has in its Theatre on Film and Tape Archive (video NCOV 2825).

[151] Kushner and Tesori, *Caroline, or Change*, Script NCOF+05-1, 112.

[152] Kushner and Tesori, *Caroline, or Change*, Script NCOF+05-1, 112.

EMMIE

I'm the daughter of a maid.
She stands alone where the harsh winds blow:
Salting the earth so nothing grow
Too close; but still her strong blood flow
Under ground through hidden veins,
Down from storm clouds when it rains,
Down the plains, down the high plateau,
Down the Gulf of Mexico.
Down to Larry and Emmie and Jackie and Joe.
The children of Caroline Thibodeaux.[153]

As Tesori puts it, Emmie "turns shame into ownership."[154]

Kushner rewrote some of the lyrics for the move to Broadway in April 2004. Now, Emmie does not begin by admitting that she is scared but instead extends the epilogue's meta-theatricality by posing questions to the audience in a newly composed recitative:

EMMIE

Just one last thing left unsaid:
Who was there when that statue fell?
Who knows where they put his head?
That ol' copper Nightmare Man?
Who can say what happened that night at the courthouse?
I can.[155]

Emmie confesses to being part of the beheading with more assertiveness and authority than in the previous script, though she is still afraid:

I was there that night; I saw,
I watched it topple like a tree.
We were scared to death to break the law!
Scared we'd fail, scared of jail.
But still we stayed.[156]

Following on earlier scripts, Emmie now only sings about a dream she had involving the statue, rather than it being enacted on stage. Kushner cut the lines about Emmie being happy that she is able to tell Caroline that she caused a change and replaced them with Emmie telling the audience how she told the statue to go away:

---

[153] Kushner and Tesori, *Caroline, or Change*, Script NCOF+05-1, 113.
[154] Tesori, interview by author, June 15, 2015.
[155] Kushner and Tesori, *Caroline, or Change*, 125.
[156] Kushner and Tesori, *Caroline, or Change*, 126.

And I said:

"Statue, statue, you are through!"

Statue answer: "Well, who are you?"

I said: "Evil, you got to go!"

Evil answer: "Who says so?"

I say:

"Emmie

Emmie Thibodeaux!

I'm the daughter of a maid,

in her uniform, crisp and clean!

Nothing can ever make me afraid!

You can't hold on, you Nightmare Men,

Your time is past now on your way

Get gone and never come again!

For change come fast and change come slow but

Everything changes!

And you got to go!"[157]

This leads to Jackie and Joe's entrance, and the epilogue's conclusion proceeds as it did in the Off-Broadway script, with the children owning their mother's background as they prepare for the future.

The epilogue makes Emmie a harbinger of change while still keeping a reference to an inanimate object, the statue's head. Inanimate objects feature prominently throughout Kushner's script, which also features a singing moon, a washing machine, a dryer, and a radio. More importantly, Caroline's absence in the epilogue reinforces the ultimate idea that the children will have a chance to embrace social change and benefit from it precisely because their mother chose to spend most of her day working as a maid in the basement of a white family's home so that they would have the means to grow. Caroline's absence implies that her choice will keep her forever present in her children's lives.

A Prescient Musical

In the wake of the protests against white supremacist and neo-Nazi groups in Charlottesville, Virginia, and the subsequent tragic car attack that killed one demonstrator in the summer of 2017, *The New York Times* ran an article on August 20 with the headline "Topple a Confederate Statue? This Broadway Musical Already Did." The author, Michael Paulson, invited readers to consider the relevance and prescience of *Caroline, or Change* by writing, "To revisit the show's story and lyrics is to gain another vantage point on the longstanding frustrations and impatience fueling much of today's agitation and activism over the removal of statues, flags, and street and building names that honor the

---

[157] Kushner and Tesori, *Caroline, or Change*, 126.

Confederacy."[158] The 2017 London revival opened with a bare stage, except for the Confederate statue, while the second act began with the statue's head on the ground.[159] By placing the statue physically on the stage, this revival not only highlighted this subplot but also demonstrated, as Paulson had shown, that its significance and resonance were greater in 2017 than when the musical first appeared. The musical's ability to remain topical speaks volumes about racial questions in both the USA and the UK, where intentions to topple statues of white historical figures have gone beyond Confederate figures to include those of Christopher Columbus and Winston Churchill.

Caroline, or Change reminds its audiences that moments of historical change – such as the Civil Rights Movement, the Stonewall Riots, the Equal Rights Amendment, the #MeToo Movement, the Black Lives Matter Movement, and the demands for social justice and changes in police behavior toward African Americans following the death of George Floyd in the summer of 2020, to mention just a few – reveal those who cannot embrace such change as well as those who fight for it. The situations that some African Americans (and other minorities) live simply do not afford them the possibility of change. A performance of *Caroline, or Change* affirms the lives of those who have been marginalized within liberation movements. Kushner himself has stated, "I've always been interested in people in revolutionary or protean times, when a lot of shifting is happening, who get left behind by that moment. It's a collision of the political and the personal."[160] He also confirms that in the epilogue, Emmie is "understanding her mother's sacrifices, and the strength and resistance shown by people whose resistance is not immediately identifiable as that."[161] Kushner's plot for *Caroline, or Change*, therefore, relates the conditions experienced by African American women in the 1960s to the contradictions in social justice that continue to exist in the early twenty-first century. In doing so, Kushner gives the second part of the musical's title, *Change*, yet another meaning, the one that reads as an imperative verb.

Caroline, or Change has been reimagined in productions all over the United States and always raises ongoing questions of race, justice, and social class to which American culture struggles to find answers. Its message is enhanced as it moves between speech, recitative, and song. Kushner and Tesori, in their innovative approach to musical dramaturgy, created a musical that challenged

[158] Michael Paulson, "Topple a Confederate Statue? This Broadway Musical Already Did," *New York Times*, August 20, 2017.

[159] Ian Shuttleworth, "A Thrilling Revival of *Caroline, or Change* at the Playhouse Theatre, London," *Financial Times*, December 18, 2018.

[160] Quoted in Paulson, "Topple a Confederate Statue?"

[161] Quoted in Paulson, "Topple a Confederate Statue?"

not only the book musical's balance of speaking and singing but also issues of representation and race ideology, not unlike Finn's *Falsettos* did with gender in 1992. As signs of progress slowly begin to emerge, a work like *Caroline, or Change* – similar to Lorraine Hansberry's *A Raisin in the Sun* or August Wilson's *Fences* – comes along and asks us how far we have come and whether this is far enough.

6 "We Sing It Anyway": The Sung-Through Musical in the Early Twenty-First Century

The idea of effacing the differences between book and lyrics in a sung-through musical reached a pinnacle in 2016 when Lin Manuel Miranda's (b. 1980) *Hamilton* became a cultural phenomenon. After the musical received a record-breaking sixteen nominations for that year's Tony Awards, *New York Times* critic Charles Isherwood made a comment that revealed how blurry that distinction had become by the mid-2010s: "I do find it slightly puzzling that [*Hamilton*] was nominated in the book of a musical category, since the show is almost sung-through, but it's the kind of juggernaut that we haven't seen in years."[162] Isherwood's comment was easily counterargued not just because Miranda won the Tony Award for best book of a musical that year but also because the Dramatist Guild of America was quick to respond a week later with a letter to the editor of *The New York Times* confirming that the blurring of book and lyrics exist, but these are nonetheless different crafts, and both are essential to the sung-through structure. The letter included James Lapine's words, "If anything, a sung-through musical demands even more from the book writer" whose job is to realize "how collectively . . . songs add up to a satisfying piece of storytelling," and Marsha Norman's almost aphorism, "If there is story, there is book, even if no one says a single sentence."[163]

Twenty-first-century sung-through musicals, such as Jason Robert Brown's *The Last Five Years* (2001) and Anaïs Mitchell's *Hadestown* (2016, Off-Broadway; 2019, Broadway), among others, continue to challenge the book musical's traditional structure. They do so by either performing song after song (as in Finn's *Falsettos*) or not clearly delineating where songs begin and end (as in LaChiusa's *Hello Again* or Tesori's *Caroline, or Change*) in what has become a defining aesthetic of the postmillennial American musical.

---

[162] Michael Paulson, Scott Heller, and Charles Isherwood, "'Hamilton' Aside, Where the Real Tony Competition Lies," *New York Time*, May 3, 2016.

[163] Quoted in Doug Wright, "Writing the Book for a Musical: A Misunderstood Art," Letter to the Editor, *New York Times*, May 10, 2016.

The Last Five Years

With music, lyrics, and the book by Jason Robert Brown (b. 1970), *The Last Five Years* is a one-act musical with fourteen songs, some of which include short spoken monologues, and only two characters. When asked if the musical had a book, Brown replied:

> It depends how you define book. There's not a lot of dialogue. There's a very strong structural element – which is what I sort of consider a book to be – which I created. It could be said to function like a song cycle, but it's not quite that cut and dried. One person sings, and another person sings, and intercut within some of those songs are some monologues. It's not as straightforward as a song cycle, but the impetus was to write a song cycle – a piece for two singers and a chamber ensemble. As I went on with it, it gradually became more theatrical.[164]

Brown developed the idea for his new musical in 1999, after *Parade*, for which he created the score, had completed its run at Lincoln Center, and Thomas Cott, then artistic director of Lincoln Center, commissioned Brown to write a new musical. As Brown recalled: I was determined that my next piece would be different from *Parade* in two important respects: first, I wanted it to be small in scale – two actors, so that it could be performed in any size theater, or even a concert hall or cabaret; and second, I wanted the songs to feel like, well, songs – one person having a complete musical moment, like a track on an album, without needing dialogue to tell the story.[165]

Brown had been frustrated that it had taken him years to write *Parade*, which played for just three months. He contemplated leaving the theater business to teach, but Billy Rosenfield, senior vice president for shows and soundtracks at RCA, advised him to compose a song cycle before giving up a career in musical theater. In Brown's own words: "I started thinking: 'I'll just write a song cycle' . . . it was going to be for two people. And I thought: 'Well, this is the anti-*Parade*' . . . maybe it'll be a theater song cycle."[166] Brown conceived the idea of a couple, Jamie and Cathy, who sing about how their relationship began, changed, and ended over a period of five years. The problem was that both characters would be moving towards the same dramatic climax, a breakup, which meant that the musical would have a sorrowful ending.[167]

---

[164] Quoted in Kenneth Jones, "A Brief Encounter with Jason Robert Brown," *Playbill* 19, no. 11 (August 31, 2001), 15–16.

[165] Jason Robert Brown, *The Last Five Years: The Complete Book and Lyrics of the Musical* (Milwaukee: Applause, 2011), v.

[166] Jason Robert Brown, interview by Robin Pogrebin, in "Can the Same Old Song and Dance Be New Again?" *New York Times*, February 24, 2002.

[167] Jason Robert Brown, interview by Patrick Pacheco, February 11, 2013, Works and Process at the Guggenheim: *The Last Five Years*, New York Public Library for the Performing Arts, New York.

As Brown was crossing 69th Street to meet Cott at Lincoln Center, the idea came to him that the woman's songs should start at the end of the relationship and the man's at the beginning,[168] in a way echoing the backward storytelling of Sondheim and George Furth's *Merrily We Roll Along* (1981). This would fulfill Brown's initial idea for the project and also avoid having the characters sing too many duets. He also realized that the characters' timelines would eventually cross, and at that moment, they would sing about their wedding day, the only part of the show "when they would both be in the same moment onstage at the same time."[169]

Brown began writing in June 1999. The first music that he composed was the opening waltz, which became the first twenty measures of the score and music that also returns at key moments in the plot.[170] The first complete song was the one that ends the musical, "Goodbye Until Tomorrow/I Could Never Rescue You," which features Cathy on their first date and Jamie saying goodbye on the day he leaves her.[171] Jamie's "I Could Never Rescue You" features the opening waltz as its main theme, which creates symmetry between the two ends of the musical. Brown finished composing the score in 2001 for the Chicago opening, which took place at the Northlight Theatre on May 23 of that year. *The Last Five Years* moved to New York and opened Off-Broadway at the Minetta Lane Theatre on March 3, 2002, and closed on May 5.[172] According to Brown, he rewrote some parts of the musical during and after the Chicago run, but the show did not change much once it opened in New York.[173]

The song sequence in *The Last Five Years* operates along two dramatic lines that move in opposite directions. As Jamie sings about the couple's relationship in chronological order and Cathy sings about it in reverse, each song constitutes its own scene with a specific locale, time, and character configuration. The chronological progression of their relationship from the first to the fifth year can be traced in Table 4 if Jamie's column is read downward from songs 2 to 14 and Cathy's upwards from 14 to 1.

Both characters sing the same number of songs, and only twice do they sing together (songs 8 and 14), and only once do they sing the same song, "The Next Ten Minutes" (song 8).

---

[168] Brown, *The Last Five Years*, vi.   [169] Brown, *The Last Five Years*, vi.

[170] Brown, *The Last Five Years*, vi.   [171] Brown, *The Last Five Years*, vi.

[172] The partnership with Lincoln Center fell through after Brown's ex-wife, Theresa O'Neill, maintaining that the musical was based on her own short-lived marriage with him, threatened to sue the production. She claimed that the musical violated the terms of her and Brown's divorce agreement. After Lincoln Center announced the cancellation of the production and Brown negotiated another agreement with his ex-wife in court, some producers took the musical to the Minetta Lane Theatre (Michael Riedel, "Lawsuit KOs New Musical," *New York Post*, October 26, 2001).

[173] Brown, interview by Patrick Pacheco, February 11, 2013.

Table 4 The fourteen songs from *The Last Five Years* in fourteen scenes[174]

Cathy's Songs	Jamie's Songs
(Year Five)	(Year One)
1. Still Hurting	
	2. Shiksa Goddess
3. See I'm Smiling	
	4. Moving Too Fast
5. A Part of That	
	6. The Schmuel Song
7. A Summer in Ohio	
8. The Next Ten Minutes	
	9. A Miracle Would Happen
10. Climbing Uphill	
	11. If I Didn't Believe in You
12. I Can Do Better than That	
	13. Nobody Needs to Know
14. Goodbye Until Tomorrow/I Could Never Rescue You	
(Year One)	(Year Five)

The order of the songs reveals how Brown created dramatic action, as the characters' moods shift in opposite directions as the musical progresses. Cathy begins with somber songs in slow tempos, and Jamie with upbeat, fast songs. The most desolate song that each character sings occurs in the fifth year of the relationship and therefore at opposite ends of the musical: song 1 for Cathy (her pain after Jamie breaks up with her) and song 13 for Jamie (his confession that he can no longer continue the relationship). Conversely, two of the happiest songs occur in the middle of the musical – also the middle of the relationship – when both characters sing upbeat, fast songs (songs 6 and 7). Their relationship starts to fall apart after their wedding (song 8). Cathy sings about her hopes to maintain the relationship and the frustration caused by Jamie's behavior in her first three songs, while Jamie sings about his difficulty living in a monogamous relationship and dealing with Cathy's profitless career in his four last songs.

Another song, the diegetic "When You Come Home to Me" (not listed in Table 4) occurs in the midst of two other songs, 9 and 10, and develops the character of Cathy. She is a musical theater actress and sings it at auditions.

---

[174] I borrowed the idea for this table from a similar one provided in the program of a production of *The Last Five Years* at the Berkshire Theatre Festival that ran from June 22 to July 10, 2010.

Brown marks it to be performed as a "medium ballad à la Jerome Kern" to suggest the move from non-diegetic to diegetic singing. Song 9 focuses on Jamie after the wedding struggling with monogamy, while, as a cutaway, Cathy auditions for a job in Ohio and sings the song "simply and perfectly."[175] Song 10 takes place before the wedding and depicts Cathy struggling with her career. She opens the scene with the refrain of "When You Come Home to Me," which Brown indicates to be sung "dancy and perky," thus reflecting an early approach Cathy had toward her audition song. This segues to the non-diegetic song of the scene, "Climbing Uphill." At her next audition, which takes place in the middle of the same song, Cathy thinks about her life choices and uses the diegetic song's music to reveal what is in her mind as she auditions. She becomes anxious and sings in a fast patter. The scene also features two spoken monologues delivered by Jamie and concludes with Cathy singing "When You Come Home to Me" once more, now with more intensity as she attempts, according to Brown's directions, to "compensate for her previous mousiness with a hysterical stridency, which essentially forces her to scream every note at the loudest possible volume."[176] "When You Come Home to Me" details Cathy's development as a struggling actress, albeit in reverse chronological order. She sings it as a successful audition piece in song 9 and as someone grappling with the audition process and her own life choices in song 10.

Even if it is not a strict song cycle but a piece of theater, *The Last Five Years* employs the song-cycle structure discussed previously in Finn's sung-through scores and therefore shares structural similarities to these works from the 1980s and 1990s. By contrast, the handful of spoken monologues are enough to give the musical the character of being nearly sung-through, like *Rent*. The result is a very intimate musical, whose unusualness made Brown himself, when the show first opened in Chicago, describe it as "the least likely musical I could possibly have conceived."[177]

The 2010s

Although the book musical prevailed, some of the most successful musicals of the 2010s employed and/or expanded the sung-through structures discussed so far. One especially notable development for the sung-through musical was its partnership with popular music from outside the theater, which resulted in what Jonathan Mandell called "sung-through musicals that feel more like staged concerts." This practice grew out of producing staged versions of concept

[175] Brown, *The Last Five Years*, 39.   [176] Brown, *The Last Five Years*, 47–48.
[177] Jason Robert Brown, "The Secret to My Success," *Stagebill: The Last Five Years* at Northlight Theatre (May 2001), 26.

albums, which began with Andrew Lloyd Webber and Tim Rice's *Jesus Christ Superstar* in the early 1970s.[178]

American Idiot (2010), a stage adaptation of the punk rock band Green Day's eponymous 2004 concept album, exemplifies the album-to-stage trend. In addition to the album, the score includes songs from Green Day's then recent album *21st-Century Breakdown* and the single "When It's Time." The band conceived both albums as rock operas, following the lead of The Pretty Things's *S.F. Sorrow* (1968) and The Who's *Tommy* (1969), the latter of which became a stage musical that played on Broadway from 1993 to 1995. The reliance on the albums was so strong that along with the musical *Fela!* (with songs of Fela Anikulapo-Kuti), *American Idiot* was not eligible for a Tony nomination for best score, since less than half of the score was actually written for the theater. Billie Joe Armstrong (b. 1972), Green Day's vocalist and guitarist, and Michael Mayer's (b. 1960) book tells the story of three young men coming of age in post-9/11 United States. The songs reveal more about the character's minds and inner conflicts than their intentions and actions. The only snippets of the spoken word occur between some songs when the protagonist, Johnny, writes in his journal about fleeing life in the suburbs and what he encounters in the city. As exemplified by Green Day's performance at the 2010 Tony Awards, *American Idiot* continued *Rent*'s goal to erase the line between show tunes and pop music and between Broadway musicals and rock concerts.

Another example is *The Total Bent* (2016), created by Stew (b. 1961) and Heidi Rodewald, who together had also composed the rock musical *Passing Strange* (2007). This is the story of a preacher and his son, Marty, in 1960s Alabama. A very talented young songwriter, Marty for years composed songs that helped his father become a gospel star and saved him from the fiasco of claiming himself to be a faith healer. Their relationship becomes complicated when Byron Blackwell, a British producer, offers Marty a career away from his father's shadow and also becomes Marty's lover. As a critic put it, *The Total Bent* is about "God, the Civil Rights Movement, the music industry, sexuality, and a haunted microphone."[179] The plot does not develop chronologically but rather through fragmentary recollections of Marty's past. The sung-through structure comes from the onstage band moving from song to song as characters interact with each other, the band, and the audience. Despite the high quality of the music and lyrics and a number of powerful performances, the reception of *The Total Bent* echoed the criticism accorded to previous sung-through rock

---

[178] Jonathan Mandell, "Sung-Through: Real American Musicals or Concerts with Benefits," *HowlRound*, June 2, 2016, www.howlround.com/sung-through.

[179] David Gordon, "Reviews: The Total Bent," *TheaterMania*, May 25, 2016, www.theatermania.com/new-york-city-theater/reviews/the-total-bent_77205.html.

scores like *Jesus Christ Superstar* and *Rent*, namely, that the plot is confusing and asks the audience to connect too many dots without any assistance. However, this nebulous atmosphere, which is enhanced through the continuous sung-through score, may have been precisely what the creators wanted, even to the point of having critics describe it as an experience, with the *New York Times* critic calling it "an ecstatic combination of revival meeting and rock concert."[180] Mandell provided an insightful connection between this approach and the technology and social media surrounding its audience:

> The rise of YouTube, Vimeo, Twitter, and Instagram have created a new language of perception for its users as surely as early twentieth century audiences started learning the new language of film. We quickly have gotten used to little self-contained drops of "content" – sometime concentrated wit or wisdom – that merge into an ever-moving stream of drops that may or may not be connected to one another; may or may not provide a larger context.[181]

While rock-based sung-through musicals may lack dramatic cohesion, they do attest as to how musical theater can embrace social and cultural changes (as in *Caroline, or Change*) and attract young generations to the theater.[182]

Natasha, Pierre, and the Great Comet of 1812 (2012) shifted the sung-through musical from a concert-like experience toward immersive theater. In both its on and off Broadway runs, the theater became a very large nineteenth-century Russian tearoom, with chandeliers, oil paintings, and tables with candles for the audience. Instead of one main stage, many small ones crisscrossed the house; runaways and ramps permitted the cast to perform throughout the auditorium and interact with the audience, which thus occupied meta-theatrical space as part of the cabaret-style atmosphere and performance they were attending. Dave Malloy (b. 1976) wrote music, lyrics, and the book for this musical that drops the audience in the middle of one of the plots from Tolstoy's *War and Peace*. The dramatic action develops in a song-cycle structure, although several songs are musical scenes with sung dialogue and/or the chorus either narrating the action or describing characters, plot events, and even stage directions. If the concert-like experience of *American Idiot* and *The Total Bent*

---

[180] Charles Isherwood, "In 'The Total Bent', a Father-Son Rift and a Sensational Score," *New York Times*, June 12, 2016.

[181] Mandell, "Sung-Through: Real American Musicals or Concerts with Benefits."

[182] *Jesus Christ Superstar* also participated in the decade's trend of combining musical theater with rock concert. Lloyd Webber launched an "arena tour" in 2012, whose first performance took place at the O2 Arena. NBC aired a semi-staged live concert production of *Jesus Christ Superstar* on Easter Sunday, April 1, 2018, with active participation of the audience and interactions with the performers. Both productions also emphasized connections between musical theater and pop/rock music, with Tim Minchin, Melanie Chisholm (known as Melanie C), John Legend, Sara Bareilles, and Alice Cooper in the principal roles.

may leave the audience scratching their heads to understand parts of the plot, Rachel Chavkin's direction and immersive agenda left no question unanswered, as characters entered from all sides of the theater (including the mezzanine) to make sure that the audience is following this "complicated Russian novel." As set designer Mimi Lien, who was primarily responsible for creating the musical's distinctive environment, put it, "It's not so much a show that you sit back and watch from a distance, but it's an experience that you're actually inside of."[183] Malloy reserves the only line of spoken dialogue for the musical's final scene when Pierre consoles Natasha in their only scene together, immediately before the comet passes. This dramatic context gives the spoken line strength in a sung-through score, not unlike Kushner and Tesori's spoken passages in *Caroline, or Change*. At the climax of the musical, as in *Rent*, singing is no longer enough to express their feelings, so the protagonists must resort to speaking.

Murder Ballad (2012) marks another example of immersive sung-through musical. It expands the eponymous genre of popular balladry into a piece of musical theater, here with a homicide and a tragic ending. Julia Jordan's book tells the story of Sara and the love triangle in which she finds herself after leaving downtown Manhattan to become a wife and mother uptown, and then having an affair with her ex-boyfriend. Singer-songwriter Juliana Nash wrote the music and lyrics, which rely heavily on pop-rock idioms. Director Trip Cullman and set designer Mark Wendland transformed The Manhattan Theatre Club's Studio at Stage II (an Off-Broadway theater) into a bar with tables and chairs for use by the audience members, a pool table, and a small stage for the band. The bar was open to the public before the show started, and the four characters sat among the audience members during the performance.

Nash's score blends a series of songs, some of which recur, with short passages of underscored spoken dialogue. "Prattle," for instance, is heard six times. "Narrator" appears eleven times, as it interrupts the plot and score to provide essential information, comment on the action, or remind the audience that someone will die by the end of the story. Although the role of the narrator is rooted in balladry, as a character in this musical, she has parallels to Mark in *Rent*, the various narrative comments and interactions with the audience in *Great Comet* and *The Total Bent*, as well as adult Alison in *Fun Home*, Aaron Burr in *Hamilton*, and Hermes in *Hadestown*. These multiple occurrences suggest that sung narrative interference may be a necessary, or at least practical, dramatic device in sung-through musicals as a means of simply telling the story.

---

[183] Quoted in Michael Paulson, "How to Keep the 'Great Comet' Party Going on Broadway: Dish Out the Pierogies (and Add Josh Groban)," *New York Times*, September 14, 2016.

Jeanine Tesori returned to the sung-through format in *Fun Home* (2013). Based on Alison Bechdel's graphic novel of the same name, this musical centers on the author's discovery of her sexuality while dealing with her closeted father. Lisa Kron penned the lyrics and a book that present the protagonist, Alison, in three phases of her life: childhood, college years, and adult comic strip writer. Adult Alison narrates the action as she reflects on her past and tries to see her relationship with her parents from their perspectives. The musical's structure follows that of *Caroline, or Change*, namely, having songs interspersed with brief spoken dialogue, underscoring, and a constant alternation of spoken and sung lines. Director Sam Gold joined the creative team because he admired the process of adapting a graphic novel into a musical and also how Kron and Tesori were moving away from the conventions of the book musical: "[They] never relied on convention to tell the story, [they] were constantly inventing the form as [they] wrestled with the material."[184] Kron recalls that blurring the differences between lyrics and book occurred during the compositional process, explaining the nearly sung-through structure of *Fun Home*: "I had to learn ... that lyrics are not dialogue set to music. It's hard to say exactly what they are; it's a bit mysterious. But in our early days working together, I'd hand Jeanine a page of writing, and she'd scan through it murmuring, 'not a lyric ... not a lyric ... not a lyric' and then she'd circle a pair of lines and say, 'that's a lyric'."[185] The musical's distinctive structure also caught the attention of critics. David Rooney, for example, wrote, "While the melodic stretches of Tesori's *Fun Home* score are interspersed with almost as many abstract passages or semi-spoken songs, it's the organic fusion of these elements with the domestic drama that makes it so affecting."[186]

The smash hit and cultural phenomenon *Hamilton* (2015) confirmed the success of the sung-through musical in the 2010s. Lin-Manuel Miranda wrote music, lyrics, and the book for the show as well as originating its title character. Miranda's score unfolds from song to song as it tells the story of Alexander Hamilton from his childhood to his death in a duel with Aaron Burr. The majority of songs enact the dramatic action through rap music, which by definition employs rhythmic and rhyming speech, thus enabling Miranda to pack an immense number of words, information, and dramatic action in the course of a single song. Miranda has claimed that the musicals that influenced him during his compositional process were *Jesus Christ Superstar, Les*

---

[184] Sam Gold, Lisa Kron, and Jeanine Tesori, interview published in the souvenir program for the original Broadway run of *Fun Home*, 9.

[185] Gold, Kron, and Tesori, interview published in the souvenir program for the original Broadway run of *Fun Home*, 9.

[186] David Rooney, "*Fun Home*: Theater Review," *Hollywood Reporter*, April 19, 2015.

Misérables, and *Rent*, all sung-through musicals.[187] As with Finn and Larson, the sung-through format developed naturally since Miranda started the project with songs. The opening number, "Alexander Hamilton," was the first music that he composed for a concept album-like project then titled *The Hamilton Mixtape*. Miranda famously performed the song at Barack Obama's White House in 2009, which resulted in Miranda becoming a YouTube sensation and introducing many of his fans to the project. "My Shot" was the second song that Miranda composed, and the one that inspired him and Tommy Kail (who directed *Hamilton*) to turn the project into a stage musical.[188] Having started the project with songs, Miranda realized that the singing could not stop. He said, "If you start with our opening number, you can't go back to speech. The ball is thrown too high in the air."[189] *Hamilton* has just one scene near the end of Act I that is not musicalized or sung. Miranda has said that he did it on purpose: being a spoken scene, it would not be included on the cast recording and therefore create a surprise for audience members familiar with the score when they saw the musical onstage.[190]

Anaïs Mitchell (b. 1981) began working on *Hadestown* thirteen years before it opened on Broadway in 2019. The project started as a song cycle that Mitchell performed to the positive response in 2006 and 2007. It became a concept album in 2010, and Mitchell began the process of turning it into a stage musical. She rewrote, cut, and added songs as *Hadestown* was performed Off-Broadway at the New York Theatre Workshop (2016), the Citadel Theatre (Edmonton, Alberta, 2017), and the National Theatre (London, 2018). The story is a modern retelling of the ancient myth of Orpheus and Eurydice, mixed with that of Persephone, queen of the underworld and embodiment of spring. Set in a dystopian and depressive time period with sounds and visual touches of a deceased New Orleans, Hades's underworld is an Orwellian industrial place to which a hungry and desperate Eurydice escapes, while Orpheus focuses on his songwriting.

Mitchell sees her work as poetry first, which is then transformed into song. When asked what her priorities were when composing, she explained: "It's

---

[187] Jonathan Franks, "Lin-Manuel Miranda Opened Up About *Hamilton*, His Musical History and Hip-Hop Influences," *Inquisitr: News Worth Sharing*, May 8, 2016, www.inquisitr.com /3077264/lin-manuel-miranda-opened-up-about-hamilton. For parallels between *Hamilton* and *Les Misérables*, see Jeffrey Magee, "Miranda's *Les Miz*," *Studies in Musical Theatre* 12, no. 2 (2018): 213–21.

[188] Lin-Manuel Miranda and Jeremy McCarter, *Hamilton: The Revolution* (New York: Grand Central, 2016), 21–22.

[189] Quoted in Franks, "Lin Manuel Opened Up About *Hamilton*."

[190] Nora Dominick, "*Hamilton*'s Lin-Manuel Miranda Shares a Scene Not on the Cast Album," *Broadway World*, September 24, 2015, www.broadwayworld.com/article/HAMILTONs-Lin-Manuel-Miranda-Shares-a-Scene-Not-on-the-Cast-Album-20150924.

poetry for me. It's the rhymes and the lines and them sounding right coming out of someone's mouth. ... *Hadestown* is mostly sung through, and all of the dialogue rhymes ... it's metered and it's underscored."[191] Her background as a singer-songwriter also played a considerable role in the sung-through structure of the musical. Similar to Finn and Larson, Mitchell has found songs to be an effective method to fill in narrative gaps between her characters' more introspective moments: "I come from the songwriting world, and sort of how to write a three-and-a-half-minute song is what I knew how to do. And then I'd say working on the book of this thing has just been figuring out how to make those songs tell the story in a moment-to-moment way."[192] Examples that connect full-blown songs and develop the dramatic action include Hermes's narrative interventions and Orpheus's song, "Epic," which occurs at several instances throughout the musical as he struggles to compose his song and eventually performs for Hades, along with several song reprises.

The musical's final utterance connects to the show's sung-through structure. Hermes confirms that this is a tragic story, one that has been told before, and like Persephone comes back every year bringing new flowers and hope, so does the story gets recounted again and again, "as if it might turn out this time." The musical's finale, thus, explains – in a meta-theatrical way – why they tell that story and "sing it anyway."

In the early twenty-first century, sung-through musicals have become more of a norm rather than occasional curiosities. Yet no two function in exactly the same way. Whether the form works for a chronologically innovative plot as in *The Last Five Years*, a concept album-turned-stage musical like *American Idiot*, a piece of immersive theatre like *Natasha, Pierre, and the Great Comet of 1812*, a song-cycle retelling of classical myth such as *Hadestown*, or something else, the sung-through musical format offers audiences the chance to experience theatrical worlds in new and highly engaging ways.

Epilogue: "What's This Cheery Singing All About?"

In Kim Kowalke's article "Theorizing the Golden Age Musical: Genre, Structure, Syntax," the author breaks apart the musico-dramatic conventions that formed and structured musicals from 1943 to 1968. He shows that the book musical is "a dramaturgical model relatively stable in its generic conventions"

---

[191] Quoted in Ruthie Fierberg, "Tony Nominees Chad Beguelin, Scott Brown, Robert Horn, Bob Martin, Anaïs Mitchell, and Dominique Morisseau Talk Challenges and Triumphs of Writing a Musical," *Playbill*, June 4, 2019, www.playbill.com/article/tony-nominees-chad-beguelin-scott-brown-robert-horn-bob-martin-anais-mitchell-and-dominique-morisseau-talk-challenges-and-triumphs-of-writing-a-musical.

[192] Quoted in Fierberg, "Tony Nominees."

and it features "generic codes of signification common to the shared syntax of the Golden Age musical."[193] Jack Viertel, in his empirical examination of "how Broadway shows are built," unpacks the template that "proved a fertile one for Broadway shows that have stood the test of time" and their "common set of rules for construction."[194] Both reveal and analyze similarities in narrative structure, character types, and song functions that unify different musicals under the same genre, and audiences learn to recognize and, over time, expect.

This Element has shown a wide variety of structures and processes within the sung-through format in both Off-Broadway and Broadway musicals, revealing not just how the conventions and the template of the book musical, exemplified by Rodgers and Hammerstein, can be reworked and repurposed but also how the sung-through musical creates its own "generic codes of signification," "rules for construction," or aesthetics. In the span of four decades, different creative teams devised techniques and methods that both arise from and construct the dramaturgy of sung-through musicals.

Some of these techniques and methods are rooted in the inception of the musical's compositional process and the intuitiveness of the composers. Both Galt MacDermot and Jeanine Tesori first received a complete libretto, or a play in verse, which they were expected to set entirely to music as in an opera, and both took liberties to adapt lyrics, which characters sing which passages and even the plot accordingly so that their sung-through musicals were not musical settings of words but coherent compositions. Andrew Lippa's *Wild Party* was not that different. Instead of a play, he started with March's poem as the main structure to be set to music. William Finn's musicals considered here, *American Idiot*, *Hamilton*, and *Hadestown*, are sung-through musicals created out songs. If Sheldon Harnick once opined that the book is what comes first in a musical,[195] the compositional process of these works proves that starting out with songs around which a plot is conceived can also be a viable preliminary step toward musical theater composition. To boot, following the practice that Andrew Lloyd Webber and Tim Rice utilized in *Jesus Christ Superstar* and *Evita* in the 1970s, *American Idiot* and *Hadestown* were concept albums before they became stage musicals, and Lin-Manuel Miranda started writing songs for a hip-hop concept album titled *The Hamilton Mixtape*, which later became the musical *Hamilton*.[196] Finn's musicals, *Rent*, and

---

[193] Kowalke, "Theorizing the Golden Age Musical," 175.

[194] Jack Viertel, *The Secret Life of the American Musical: How Broadway Shows Are Built* (New York: Sarah Crichton Books, 2016), 10.

[195] Sheldon Harnick, "What Comes First in a Musical? The Libretto," in *Playwrights, Lyricists, and Composers on Theater*, ed. Otis L. Guernsey, Jr. (New York: Dodd, Mead & Co., 1974), 38.

[196] Miranda and McCarter, *Hamilton*, 10. Several of the songs from the musical (including cut songs) formed the tracks of a concept album titled *The Hamilton Mixtape* that was released in 2016, after the musical's opening.

Hadestown all show that sometimes the composer or songwriter compensates for a lack of playwrighting skills with additional songs that successfully fix dramaturgical problems or gaps. Thus, some sung-through musicals reached that form accidentally (Finn's musicals and *Rent*), while for others, it was intentional (*Human Comedy, Caroline, or Change*, and *The Wild Party*).

Sung-through musicals demonstrate different ways to construct musical continuity. Some adhere to a song-cycle structure, in which the dramatic action moves from one self-contained song to another, which then begets the scenes of a sung-through musical (all of the Marvin musicals, *A New Brain, The Last Five Years, American Idiot, Natasha, Pierre and the Great Comet of 1812, Hamilton*, and *Hadestown*). Others opt for a musical architecture in which songs are interleaved with other musico-dramatic means, such as vamps, songs that are broken into sections and scattered throughout the score, songs that are prolonged throughout a scene, song fragments that do not derive from or develop into a full-blown song, musical themes that return across scenes, and underscoring upon which spoken, sung, or recitative lines occur. These techniques are observable in all of the nearly sung-through musicals discussed in Section 3, and also in *Caroline, or Change, Fun Home, Murder Ballad*, and *Hadestown*.

Yet another characteristic of sung-through musicals concerns how the musicals are experienced. As several critics have pointed out, the lack of spoken dialogue and continuous singing ask the audience to connect dramatic dots and infer the plot, which seems to weigh less than the themes and concepts the characters sing about (*Human Comedy, Rent, A New Brain, American Idiot*, and *The Total Bent*). Some sung-through musicals invite the audience to experience the performance as a live music concert (*Rent, American Idiot*, and *The Total Bent*), while others use the physical space of the theater to immerse the audience in the sung-through plot (*Natasha, Pierre, and the Great Comet of 1812* and *Murder Ballad*). Several include a narrator who provides dramatic content or context (*Rent; Natasha, Pierre, and the Great Comet of 1812; Fun Home; Murder Ballad; Hamilton; The Total Bent*; and *Hadestown*).

The sung-through musical creates a subtext that the clearer division between singing and speaking in the conventional book musical cannot achieve. This Element has shown how the ambiguity between speaking and singing can be used purposefully to develop drama or character, especially when snippets of spoken dialogue are underscored within the musical continuum. Spoken and sung passages acquire specific functions, and in several examples, the spoken stands out and opens room for interpretation on why the creators chose certain lines to be spoken (*Hello Again; Rent; The Wild Party; Caroline, or Change; Natasha, Pierre, and the Great Comet of 1812; Fun Home; Hamilton*; and *Hadestown*). Subtext also develops from how some composers shift the continuous singing from non-diegetic to diegetic (as in *Rent, The Last Five Years*, and *Caroline, or Change*) and from some creative teams' claim that singing is too non-naturalistic and good to suspend disbelief and address sensitive topics like war, racial tension, and death (as in *The Human Comedy* and *Caroline, or Change*).

All of these processes and methods designate strategies and even models to tell diverse stories, challenging the balance between singing and speaking. They show that the musicals in this Element are sufficiently similar to be categorized and recognized as a genre (or perhaps a subgenre) of musical theater.

Effacing the lines between singing and speaking also accounts for musical theater's entrance and participation in the postmodern era. One facet of post-modernism is the removal of differences between fields or spheres, and post-modern events (including art) are not experienced through one single aesthetic but through a confluence of aesthetics derived from different sources. If differences collapse, it can become easy to lose track of the references that distinguished different forms in the past, leading to a state of confusion as spectators no longer recognize what they experience.[197] Although the book musical that clearly demarcates spoken dialogue and song continues to dominate, the sung-through format from 1980 to the 2010s and its blurring of differences – between book and lyrics, sung and spoken, musical and opera, musical and rock concert, and Off- and on Broadway – demonstrate that the American musical has absorbed postmodern ideas.

Another example is the fact that sung-through musicals have entered the world of cinema and television in the first two decades of the twenty-first century. Three of the musicals discussed in this Element have been adapted to film: *Rent* (2005), *The Last Five Years* (2014), and *Hello Again* (2017). Although their receptions were not as positive as their theatrical counterparts, these adaptations widened the audience exposed to sung-through musicals. In 2008, the last performance of the original Broadway production of *Rent* was released to the public as *Rent: Filmed Live on Broadway. Hamilton* was released on *Disney+* in July 2020 for home streaming. Furthermore, several non-musical television series, in which speaking is the norm, introduced musical episodes. In "Once More, With Feeling" (2001) from *Buffy the Vampire Slayer* and "My Musical" (2007) from *Scrubs*, the characters break into song so often that they reveal the sung-through format as the rule for how musicals work; characters sing lines like "they got the mustard out" and wonder "what's this cheery singing all about?" and "why am I singing?" In both cases, singing is so

---

[197] Fredric Jameson, "The Aesthetics of Singularity," *New Left Review* 92 (April 2015): 107–15.

abnormal that there must be a reason for it to happen: in the *Scrubs* episode, it is a symptom of a patient's medical condition, and in "Once More, With Feeling," it is the result of a demonic spell. The elimination of differentiation invites audiences/spectators to experience entertainment that combines media, genres, and both musical and dramaturgical styles into new, unique postmodern encounters, of which the sung-through musical is one participant, blurring the lines among stage musicals, film, a concert of popular music, and television series.

The techniques, methods, and processes discussed in this Element and the fact that they help disclose the postmodern identity of musical theater reveal the place of the sung-through musical in the late twentieth and early twenty-first centuries, both aesthetically and ideologically. They show the musical's ability to reinvent itself and its musico-dramatic conventions, not unlike what occurred in the 1940s. One of the connections that successful musicals establish with their audiences is that when characters break into song – suspension of disbelief aside – they reflect upon and deepen aspects of the human experience. The sung-through musical has expressed this idea through various compositional techniques and approaches that give the act of singing new dimensions, forms of expression, and dramaturgical purposes. This is why they are not talking. If singing is essential in a musical, why not sing it through?

References

Archival Sources

Jonathan Larson Papers. Call No. ML31.L37. Library of Congress, Music Division, Washington, DC.

The New York Shakespeare Festival Records, 1954–1992. Call No. *T-Mss 1993–028. New York Public Library for the Performing Arts, Billy Rose Theatre Division, New York.

Secondary Sources

Bádue, Alex. "Performing Gender, Sexuality, and Jewishness in the Songs of William Finn's Musical *Falsettoland* (1990)." *Studies in American Jewish Literature* 38, no. 2 (2019): 159–78.

Bell, Marty. *Broadway Stories: A Backstage Journey through Musical Theatre.* New York: Limelight, 1993.

Block, Geoffrey. "Frank Loesser's Sketchbooks for 'The Most Happy Fella'." *The Musical Quarterly* 73, no. 1 (1989): 60–78.

Brown, Jason Robert. *The Last Five Years: The Complete Book and Lyrics of the Musical.* Milwaukee: Applause, 2011.

Clum, John. *Still Acting Gay: Male Homosexuality in Modern Drama.* Rev. ed. New York: Palgrave Macmillan, 2000.

Dietz, Dan. *Off-Broadway Musicals, 1910–2007: Casts, Credits, Songs, Critical Reception and Performance Data of More than 1800 Shows.* Jefferson, NC: McFarland, 2010.

Dumaresq, William, and Galt MacDermot. *The Human Comedy.* New York: Samuel French, 1985.

Everett, William A. "Golden Days in Old Heidelberg: The First-Act Finale of Sigmund Romberg's *The Student Prince.*" *American Music* 12, no. 3 (1994): 255–82.

Finn, William. *In Trousers.* New York: Samuel French, 1986.

The Marvin Songs, Three One-Act Musicals: In Trousers, March of the Falsettos, and Falsettoland. Garden City, NY: The Fireside Theatre, 1990.

Falsettos: March of the Falsettos and Falsettoland by William Finn and James Lapine, and In Trousers by William Finn. New York: Plume Drama, 1992.

Finn, William, and James Lapine. *A New Brain.* New York: Samuel French, 1999.

Fisher, James. *The Theater of Tony Kushner: Living Past Hope*. New York: Routledge, 2001.

Friedman, Jonathan C. *Rainbow Jews: Jewish and Gay Identity in the Performing Arts*. Lanham, MD: Lexington Books, 2007.

Furia, Philip. *Ira Gershwin: The Art of the Lyricist*. New York: Oxford University Press, 1996.

Guernsey, Otis L., Jr., ed. *Playwrights, Lyricists, Composers on Theater*. New York: Dodd, Mead & Co., 1974.

Hinton, Stephen. *Weill's Musical Theater: Stages of Reform*. Berkeley: University of California Press, 2012.

Jameson, Fredric. "The Aesthetics of Singularity." *The New Left Review* 92 (April 2015): 101–32.

Kowalke, Kim H. "Theorizing the Golden Age Musical: Genre, Structure, Syntax." *A Music-Theoretical Matrix: Essays in Honor of Allen Forte (Part V)*, edited by David Carson Berry, *Gamut* 6, no. 2 (2013): 133–84.

Kushner, Tony, and Jeanine Tesori. *Caroline, or Change*. New York: Theatre Communications Group, 2004.

LaChiusa, Michael John. *Hello Again: A Musical*. New York: Dramatists Play Service, 1995.

Larson, Jonathan. *Rent: The Complete Book and Lyrics of the Broadway Musical*. New York: Applause, 2008.

Lippa, Andrew. *The Wild Party*. New York: Musical Theatre International, 2000.

Magee, Jeffrey. "Miranda's *Les Miz*." *Studies in Musical Theatre* 12, no. 2 (2018): 213–21.

Mandelbaum, Ken. *Not Since Carrie: Forty Years of Broadway Musical Flops*. New York: St. Martin's Press, 1992.

mcclung, bruce d. *Lady in the Dark: Biography of a Musical*. New York: Oxford University Press, 2007.

McDonnell, Evelyn, and Kathy Silberger. *Rent by Jonathan Larson*. New York: Harper Entertainment, 1997.

McMillin, Scott. *The Musical as Drama*. Princeton: Princeton University Press, 2006.

Miranda, Lin-Manuel, and Jeremy McCarter. *Hamilton: The Revolution*. New York: Grand Central, 2016.

Moross, Jerome, and John Latouche. *The Golden Apple: A Musical in Two Acts*. New York: Random House, 1954.

Pollack, Howard. *The Ballad of John Latouche: An American Lyricist's Life and Work*. New York: Oxford University Press, 2017.

Rogers, Bradley. *The Song Is You: Musical Theatre and the Politics of Bursting into Song and Dance*. Iowa City: University of Iowa Press, 2020.

Singer, Barry. *Ever After: The Last Years of Musical Theater and Beyond*. New York: Applause, 2004.

Snelson, John. *Andrew Lloyd Webber*. New Haven: Yale University Press, 2004.

Stempel, Larry. *Showtime: A History of the Broadway Musical Theater*. New York: W. W. Norton, 2010.

Sternfeld, Jessica. *The Megamusical*. Bloomington: Indiana University Press, 2006.

Sternfeld, Jessica, and Elizabeth Wollman, eds. *The Routledge Companion to the Contemporary Musical*. New York: Routledge, 2020.

Suskin, Steven. *Opening Night on Broadway: A Critical Quotebook of the Golden Era of the Musical Theatre, Oklahoma! (1943) to Fiddler on the Roof (1964)*. New York: Schirmer Books, 1990.

Turan, Kenneth, and Joseph Papp. *Free for All: Joe Papp, the Public, and the Greatest Theater Story Ever Told*. New York: Doubleday, 2009.

Viertel, Jack. *The Secret Life of the American Musical: How Broadway Shows Are Built*. New York: Sarah Crichton Books, 2016.

Acknowledgments

Research for this project was partially funded by the Presser Foundation.

Musical Theatre

William A. Everett

University of Missouri-Kansas City

William A. Everett, PhD is Curators' Distinguished Professor of Musicology at the University of Missouri-Kansas City Conservatory, where he teaches courses ranging from medieval music to contemporary musical theatre. His publications include monographs on operetta composers Sigmund Romberg and Rudolf Friml and a history of the Kansas City Philharmonic Orchestra. He is a contributing co-editor of the *Cambridge Companion to the Musical* and the *Palgrave Handbook of Musical Theatre Producers*. Current research topics include race, ethnicity and the musical and London musical theatre during the 1890s.

About the Series

Elements in Musical Theatre focus on either some sort of "journey" and its resulting dialogue, or on theoretical issues. Since many musicals follow a quest model (a character goes in search of something), the idea of a journey aligns closely to a core narrative in musical theatre. Journeys can be, for example, geographic (across bodies of water or land masses), temporal (setting musicals in a different time period than the time of its creation), generic (from one genre to another), or personal (characters in search of some sort of fulfilment). Theoretical issues may include topics relevant to the emerging scholarship on musical theatre from a global perspective and can address social, cultural, analytical, and aesthetic perspectives.

Cambridge Elements ≡

Musical Theatre

Elements in the Series

Printed in the United States
by Baker & Taylor Publisher Services